Theology of the Womb

Theology of the Womb

KNOWING GOD THROUGH THE BODY OF A WOMAN

❦

Christy Angelle Bauman

FOREWORD BY
Dan and Becky Allender

CASCADE *Books* · Eugene, Oregon

THEOLOGY OF THE WOMB
Knowing God Through the Body of a Woman

Cascade Books
An Imprint of Wipf and Stock Publishers
199 W. 8th Ave., Suite 3
Eugene, OR 97401

www.wipfandstock.com

PAPERBACK ISBN: 978-1-5326-6217-1
HARDCOVER ISBN: 978-1-5326-6218-8
EBOOK ISBN: 978-1-5326-6219-5

Cataloguing-in-Publication data:

Names: Bauman, Christy Angelle, author.
Title: Theology of the womb : knowing God through the body of a woman / Christy
     Angelle Bauman.
Description: Eugene, OR: Cascade Books, 2019 | Includes bibliographical references and
     index.
Identifiers: ISBN 978-1-5326-6217-1 (paperback) | ISBN 978-1-5326-6218-8 (hardcover) |
     ISBN 978-1-5326-6219-5 (ebook)
Subjects: LCSH: Body image in women—Religious aspects—Christianity. | Christian
     women—Religious life. | Self-acceptance in women—Religious aspects—Christianity.
Classification: BV4527 .B40 2019 (print) | BV4527 (ebook)

Manufactured in the U.S.A.   DECEMBER 5, 2019

DEDICATION

To my Mema,
Rosemarie Marks Jackson,
for our lifetime of conversations in your kitchen rocking chairs.
Sono in debito con te donna saggia.

To my sisterhood, with whom I buried and birthed,
Each of you are *mes femmes sage*
Et
à ma famille, de qui je suis venu.

To every woman in search of the *imago Dei* within herself,
may you find Her.

We each bear the song of the Savior within our wombs. Women have borne the weight of silence in the church since the beginning of time, disappearing as we groan on all fours, ushering life into this aging world. There are few women who have broken through Christianity's glass ceiling, as it relates to our gender. The female has been required to remain submissive, bleed, and bear. We wear our breasts like hidden shields of shame rather than a breastplate of righteousness. Our wombs, though muffled, can still be heard. If we pause and listen, one might hear the faint, but victorious rumble rooted in the earth's soil.

"I am woman, imago Dei, an image bearer of God, chosen to carry a message of creation, death, and ultimately ever-bearing life."

CHRISTY ANGELLE-VIDRINE BAUMAN
SEATTLE, WASHINGTON

Table of Contents

Foreword

Dear Bold Reader,

It seemed wise to write this foreword as a letter. This book is so profoundly intimate, thoughtful, and life-changing that it seems ill-conceived to use a "normal" structure. As a man, I don't enter the Red Tent—it is a holy space that is not mine to inhabit. However, I have spent too many decades of my life grateful that I am not allowed into that realm. I confess, however, that I shudder deep in my bones at the thought of walking into any sacred space. There is something foreign, dangerous, and alluring that I resist as I return to "trade bleared, smeared with toil." I prefer the daylight of the ordinary to the dark unknown of mystery. Also, I don't.

Christy invites me, a man, to stand at the threshold of what I will never suffer, or birth; what I will never know as a loss or a privileged joy. She invites me to behold, wait in mystery, and let the smell of life fill me with desire. There are realities I will never grasp or comprehend as a man, but as a human being, I am meant to receive and to hold in awe. This labor of love is an invitation into the heart of God our mother.

Christy addresses our reluctance, if not fear and, for some, revulsion, to conceive of God as a mother. She doesn't resolve the biblical or theological issues, but she calls me to remember my grandmother and at least to wonder why the being of God who is neither male nor female is not seen through the experience of the feminine as much as through the lens of the masculine.

Studies have shown that women read more than men, especially in areas that make men feel uncomfortable. I fear that few men will read this book. I suspect that most readers will be women and I strongly urge you to ask your partner or friend to read this book with you. Tell him it will not only help him know your suffering and joy with higher intensity, but will enable you both to embrace sex, gender, and mystery with greater pleasure.

Most importantly, this book opens to us all a way to share the glory of love as we are born into the delight of God. We are loved. God loves us beyond what we can name or embrace. I closed this book and thanked my grandmother for being the face of God. My beloved wife will finish our letter to you.

Beloved Reader,

Dan is a man who knows more about the heart of a woman than any other man I have ever known. However, he is correct: he has not been in nor will he ever be invited into the Red Tent. It is a sisterhood that knows a monthly process that brings either a loss of hope or relief, for some a lifetime loss of never having a full womb, and for others a bitter loss of the miscarriage or stillborn. Also, for many a weight of glory that is more than we can ever fathom. It is physically, socially, economically, and spiritually complex to be a woman. It always has been.

What I found as I read Christy's holy and beautiful book is coming home to my body. There are so many voices that delegitimize a woman's experience, especially as we age. When I walk into a nice store to look for clothes, salespeople don't see me. It is as if the female clerk doesn't know what to do with an aging face and body. I am a reminder to younger women what will one day happen to the beauty of their body. I am invisible to men and, I am a reminder to younger women. As I read Christy's book, I was reminded of my scars and the warfare of infertility, miscarriages, leakage, seepage, pain, and far, far more joy. I love being a woman, and yet it is and has always been something far more complex than what it seems my husband suffers. There is no point to compare the cost of living in a fallen world, but Christy's work allowed me to enter what it means as a woman to be "fearfully and wonderfully made." I regretted not having this book when I was a young woman, and I can assure you that my daughters, daughter-in-law, and granddaughters will receive this book as a present. I, too, hope my son and every other man I love will read as well. *Theology of the Womb* is a gift I trust you will receive and offer to everyone you love.

Dan and Becky Allender
Bainbridge Island, Washington
February 20, 2019

Preface

MY MOMMA TELLS ME that when I was still in her womb, she would go to prayer meetings for Catholics who were prophetic. In one of those meetings, it was prophesied that I would lead the assemblies in praise. She would always reminisce on their words. "*Christy, they said you would lead the congregations in worship and singing . . .*" Spoiler alert: I rarely sing in public. I have a pretty good singing voice, but I lack the faith or naiveté needed to be a worship leader. What I do have, however, is a stubborn gift of hope, and I am a better author than worship leader. Either way, my passion runs deep, and I persist in my pursuits until I achieve what I set out to accomplish.

My spiritual development was that of a passion-hungry orphan destined for a convent. When I was in middle school, I prayed for the gift of speaking in tongues. My youth pastor told me to start practicing by saying words in repetition. I practiced almost every night for a year, to no avail. I even broke up with my eighth-grade boyfriend, Luke, telling him I needed to focus on God more, but, looking back, wish I had at least kissed him a few times before radically claiming my celibacy. You see, I have always been desperate for God. In high school at a church revival, I went up to the altar call hoping that I would get slain in the Spirit, but the weight of the evangelist's hand felt heavier on my chest than the Holy Spirit power. As I rocked back and forth and was laid down on the floor, my legs covered with a blanket so as not to be inappropriate, I lay there wondering if this was really what the Holy Spirit felt like. At the ripe age of seventeen, when the Brownsville Assembly of God church in Pensacola, Florida was having a revival and "gold dust" was appearing in their services, I drove five hours by myself to see it. As I told you, I have the gift of hope, but not of faith, and I wanted to see it with my own eyes. In the midst of thousands of people,

I never saw the gold dust or laughed prophetically, but I was still an avid believer in the Spirit.

My theology of prayer was shaky by this point, with an uncertainty of how God was suppose to show up in my life, so I settled into a less charismatic and more theophostic approach, where I coined phrases like "I'm not prophetic, but am sometimes given the gift of knowledge" or "I heard/saw this while I was praying for you, does this mean anything to you?" Multiple times while visiting Africa, I remember going to places where we prayed for demons to leave and for people to come back from the dead. In my quest for understanding, I asked an African friend about his belief in this practice, to which he replied, "It isn't prayer, *it is the power of speaking words of love to combat hate.*" My prayer theology grew and began to look more like desiring good over evil, love versus hate. Although God has control over all things, God allows the tension of love and hate to co-exist in the same world.

My greatest prayers of faith were yet to come. The week before my first son was born, our congregation prayed in church for a safe delivery and healthy baby boy. My son died four days later. I remember praying over his silent body that he would breathe again. We asked people come and pray for the same thing. He didn't breathe again. My husband confessed months later that he feared whatever we prayed for, the opposite would happen. Evil and anxiety start to manifest in my heart the same way, and fear gripped me mercilessly. For a very long time, prayer became safe to me only when it was silent, or when other people prayed. Sadly, it became an obsessive-compulsive ritual that required much psychological work to amend. Prayer and relief take many forms for me now: a repetitive sign of the cross over myself, my loved ones, or my expanded belly; sometimes in watching TV after a night wrecked with anxiety or finding "holy oil" and walking through anointing the door posts in my house. Prayer looks like mornings when I quietly watch the sunrise as my children play on our living room floor and I breathe in deeply. Sometimes it is my summoning the figure of C. S. Lewis' fictitious lion character, Aslan, next to me and asking for protection. Prayer looks like calling a friend late at night who stops brushing her teeth to pray for my shaking, fearful body. Prayer sometimes comes as I repeat: *"Perfect love drives out all fear. Perfect love drives out all fear. Love drives out fear. Any love drives out any fear. Love, love, love wins."* This became the only prayer I could muster in desperate hopes of warding off a panic attack. Faith and hope are both tools we use to respond to trauma and loss, but what I advocate for is learning to practice and pursue love deeply, for love is ultimately what can heal trauma and defeat loss. Love was placed inside of your womb while you were still in utero and you are innately gifted with its power.

This is a book about pieces of my story's hunger for passion and painful trauma with God through my own emotional, spiritual, and physical body and blood. After trauma, I was long overdue to meet a God who was larger than the God I was taught about growing up. Although I had a private Christian education from preschool to PhD, my theology was lacking. It wasn't enough to grow up in a Catholic family, attend an Assemblies of God high school, and go through a Reformed seminary. It didn't suffice to be able to translate Hebrew and some Greek, speak in tongues, and give long-winded monologues over transubstantiation and infant baptism. I was not content with God because I could not find God as a woman or a mother. My research in the feminine aspects of God, the effects of sexual objectification, and the female body, were cries from my soul of what I never heard from the pulpit. I wanted to meet a part of God that resembled a woman, a God that looked something like me.

Theology of the Womb is a few stories from my own journey of finding a God who bleeds just like my body bleeds on a monthly basis. In these pages are an invitation to discover a God who will sometimes have to take on feminine pronouns to be addressed accurately. For some this text may feel blasphemous; it did for me at times. Yet through deep prayer and research, I came to see this subject as an invitation to hear a silent message that men have been unable to address as well as women can. Men cannot give birth, and while men co-create with God as like women do, the physical act of bleeding and birthing—being intimately connected and co-creating alongside our Maker—is a part of our glory as women. May these words awaken and invite a God who embodied himself as fully woman when he created Eve. This book is deeply painful at times, as blood comes when there is both life and death. Bless your journey as you seek your own knowing of a God who created you in the *imago Dei* . . . in her own image. Please note, I will not refer to myself as feminist in this book; rather, I have come to align more with the term *womanist*. Womanism is defined as a form of feminism that emphasizes women's natural contribution to society and is used by some in distinction to the term *feminism* and its association with primarily white women.

Acknowledgments

THIS TEXT WOULD NOT be without many hands holding up my arms. First, to my partner in this world, Andrew, thank you, good man, you inspire me to dream and to go after those dreams. I love you and thank you, even at this moment as I type, and you are caring for our children—what a good, good man you are.

Second, to the women of sisterhood in my life, who I feel are cheering me on: Bonnie, Autumn, Mel, Heather, Kinsey, Lisa, Bethanne, Alyssa, Steph, Vanya, Karen, Nic, Valeska, Tran, Hayden, Cherie, Jinx, Peg, Mia, Mom, Patsy Briggs, Autherine (Ray), Nanny Janet, Mema, Libby, Neenie Shirlene, Cailee, Laurie, Nicole B., Wynn, Wendi, Julie, Tyra, Sarah, Nicole G., Aunt Shaun, the breakfast club: Toni, Angie, Beth, and April. Each of you have held me when I had no strength, dared me to create again when I had no hope, prayed for me to keep going when I had no breath. You are my kin, and I am in awe of a God who has created you and gifted you in my life.

Lastly, to those who have mentored me: Rosemarie and John Jackson, Tina Schermer Sellers, Dan and Becky Allender, Lottie Hillard, Alyssa Hahn, Melissa Roe, Jay Stringer, Ben Katt, Andy Carlson, Trapper Lukaart, Brandon and Nicole Berry, Jim and Mona Coffield, Dr. Rick Rigsby, Cher Edwards, Chris and Beth Bruno, Ray Muenich, Neva Lund, John-Paul Isbell, Nicholas Cox, Autumn Williams, Steve and Nicole Kroeger, "Pop" Mike Anthony, Tom Vidrine, Gerard Napoli, Paul and Wendy Standinger, and you, Mary Christine, my good momma, whose secure attachment and hours of holding me reminded me of God's goodness and love for me. For the beautiful endorsements, thank you Sarah Bessey, Tina Schermer Sellers, Dan and Becky Allender, Chuck DeGroat, Sharon Hersh, and Chris and Beth Bruno. To each of you, for your profound glory touching my life . . . I am ever grateful.

Acknowledgments

Thank you, Rose Gwynn Jackson, for you were not only editor but dear friend. I am grateful for you relentless combing through these words and making sense of my charismatic visions. Thank you, Ashley Tiberi, Rodney Clapp, Heather Carraher, and Shannon Carter for your editing, gifting, and expertise you offered this text.

A Litany to Honor Women from the Book of Common Prayer

WE WALK IN THE company of the women who have gone before, mothers of the faith both named and unnamed, testifying with ferocity and faith to the Spirit of wisdom and healing. They are the judges, the prophets, the martyrs, the warriors, poets, loves and saints, in the landscape of our dreams.

We walk in the company of Deborah,
who judged the Israelites with authority and strength.

We walk in the company of Esther,
who used her position as queen to ensure the welfare of her people.

We walk in the company of you whose names have been lost and silenced,
who kept and cradled the wisdom of the ages.

We walk in the company of the woman with the flow of blood,
who audaciously sought her healing and release.

We walk in the company of Mary Magdalene,
who wept at the empty tomb until the risen Christ appeared.

We walk in the company of Phoebe,
who led an early church in the empire of Rome.

We walk in the company of Perpetua of Carthage,
whose witness in the third century led her to martyrdom.

We walk in the company of St. Christian the Astonishing,
who resisted death with persistence and wonder.

We walk in the company of Julian of Norwich,
who wed imagination and theology proclaiming, "All shall be well."

We walk in the company of Sojourner Truth, who stood against oppression, righteously declaring in 1852, "Ain't I a woman!"

We walk in the company of the Argentine mothers of the Plaza de Mayo, who turned their grief to strength, standing together to remember "the disappeared" children of war with a joyful indignation.

We walk in the company of Alice Walker,
who named the lavender hue of womanish strength.

We walk in the company of you mothers of the faith,
who teach us to resist evil with boldness, to lead with wisdom, and to heal. Amen.

Introduction

The Story of the Womb

BEFORE THERE WAS A beginning, there was a womb. A womb is a place where all beginnings are created, a place where substance is generated—a deep place hidden in the void of darkness that holds the potential for the greatest act we have ever known in humankind: the creation of life. In the beginning, the very beginning, God created the heavens and the earth. The very first thing we are invited to imagine is God's womb, the place where heaven and earth were created, two places that are ever-bearing wombs, continually creating more life. The earth's womb was without form until the Spirit of God moved upon the face of the void to create: light and darkness, water and land, sunrise and sunset, plant and animal, male and female. Genesis 1 is a chronicle of the womb's greatest act, and verses 26 and 27 are the crescendo: Then God said, "Let us make human beings in *our* image, in *our* likeness, so that they may rule over the fish in the sea and the birds in the sky, over the livestock and all the wild animals, and over all the creatures that move along the ground." So, God created human beings in God's own image, *in the image of God he created them*; male and *female*, He created them. The Hebrew word for *image* is *tselem* (צֶלֶם), which means photograph, resemblance, figure, or shadow. The Latin translation is *imago Dei*, the image of God. If we had been able to observe this moment in history, we would have seen a thin veil similar to a hospital room, that we would walk through into God's birthing room. In the dusk of afternoon light, you find God and the Spirit molding clay and breathing life into their creation. I can almost hear the Spirit humming an unknown song over these beings called human life, whispering at times to God, "They look just like us, he has your chin, and she has my eyes . . . I am in awe of what we have created."

Let's not forget that we are not telling the story of creation, we are telling the story of the womb, the place in which creation was brought to gestation. The cyclical pattern of the female womb illustrates a timeline filled with wonders, anguish, and mystery. The womb is an example of the Creator who has made every creature ever-bearing.

The life cycle of the uterus mirrors the *imago Dei*, the image of God as a Creator. This Creator echoes a cycle of creation everywhere; such as the annual seasons: spring, summer, fall, and winter; the female menstrual cycles: menstrual phase, follicular phase, ovulation phase, and luteal phase; and even the church calendar: Advent/Christmas/Epiphany, Lent/Easter/Pentecost, and Ordinary Days. These are just a few examples of the cyclical pattern God continues to use throughout creation. If we view this information with a bio-psycho-spiritual understanding, we can see the female body inviting us to look at a cyclical pattern to explain concepts of spiritual, psychological, and physical interconnectedness. Through the story of the womb, perhaps your own womb, I invite you on a journey with God to explore the spiritual womb cycle: waiting/growth, creation/birth, and burial/death.

SECTION 1: Waiting and Growth

1

A Bleeding God

The great mother whom we call *Innana*
gave a gift to women that is not known among men,
and this is the secret of blood.
The flow at the dark of the moon,
the healing blood of the moon's birth—to men,
this is flux and distemper, bother and pain.
They imagine we suffer and consider themselves lucky.
We do not disabuse them.

—Anita Diamant, *The Red Tent*

Still Sneaking Tampons

It is the last blazing hot weekend in the Pacific Northwest, and our annual church camping trip is nestled in a large campground between the beautiful mountain ranges just north of Seattle. My family of four is unloading our camping gear at our chosen campsite. The kids are playing around the campground while my husband and I are putting up the new tent, miraculously without a bickering word. Our pastor's wife and decade-old friend Cherie walks over to me and whispers in my ear, "Do you have any tampons? I just started my period." I walk to the car and rummage through the glove compartment. I am still breastfeeding, but my period came back about a month ago, so I am pretty sure I have something stashed away. Hidden by the covering palm of my hand, I carry and pass the tampons off like a drug exchange. She has no pockets in her running clothes, so she slides the tampons into her sports bra. We smile knowingly and continue talking about other things. My husband comments from behind an almost assembled tent, "What are you both doing?" His inquiry is playful, but forthright. I am well aware he is awaiting my return and needs my help. Cherie and I giggle, and he smirks with a ridiculous comment, "Oh, well the secret is out, I am telling all the guys that Cherie is on her period." We all laugh and begin talking about how women have typically silenced and hidden their menstrual cycles. The conversation becomes insatiable as we exchange countless stories about embarrassing moments of bleeding that we have carried silently for years. As thirty-seven-year-old women, Cherie and I have each birthed three babies, yet the narrative of our period is still so quieted, especially within the church. We have tiptoed around the subject as if it will disgust and infringe upon others to know that we are bleeding. I ponder this silence throughout the weekend and I wonder why I feel so embarrassed about something so natural and normal. Even at a church function, with my closest friends and women I have walked alongside through pregnancies, how is it there isn't much of a theology taught about our bleeding bodies? In particular, I find our wombs actually invite us to know God as the creator in a way no other human is invited to know God. When I push past the embarrassment, I am in awe of how God is telling a story through the body of woman and the womb that brings a soul into this world. How tragic that we have turned away from our bodies in shame and hidden this expression of the gospel. We desperately need to turn toward our bleeding and bearing bodies with kindness and curiosity, and bless them. It would behoove us to study the theology that is being displayed in a woman's womb.

Twenty-two years after my first period, I am only beginning to have open conversations about menstrual cycles. Although Cherie and I are no longer embarrassed about carrying tampons and scrounging for feminine products from each other, we must be intentional to nuance and not keep our bleeding a secret from men and from the world. My six-year-old son, Wilder, and four-year-old daughter, Selah, have had many questions already in their childhood, such as who is where on the food chain sort of questioning. They want to know their place as they realize there is a difference between boys and girls; they are seeking to deepen their understanding of dominance between genders. Whether in public or private, with friends or strangers, television shows, or sporting events, they cheer for the person who is their same gender. Often male competitors were more prominent in sports, and their wins would leave my daughter in tears, to her brother's delight. Selah would often ask me, "Mom, where are all the girls?" I have often asked myself the same questions, not only with sports, but usually when I am reading the Bible.

In the Bible, the stories of women mostly present imagery of the woman's beauty as sexual, and their value is measured in terms of their reproductivity, specifically as it applies to bearing male children. I have yet to read a Bible passage on lineage that has more than one woman's name in it. Even though it is a woman's body that births humans, their names don't make it into the passages on bloodlines. The few women who are named in the Bible are categorized as either virgins, promiscuous, mothers, infertile, widowed, or temple prostitutes. Biblical women prided themselves on birthing males for their husband, even though, physiologically, it is the man's sperm that determines the sex of the child. The patriarchal era of men being more valuable than women is slowly fading, allowing for some advocacy for equal worth amongst all humankind, regardless of gender or skin color. We can still see this mindset lingering globally, such as in China's one-child policy that has only recently changed to a two-child policy; civil rights laws are only decades old; and refugee and gender laws that are still controversial. So, when my daughter asks, "Where are all the women?" and the biblical text has no female deity, I am left with a similar wondering. A biblical woman's reproductivity is often seen as her dominant career or calling, and her menstrual cycles as something to be avoided. Scripture literally mandates that a menstruating woman must "go outside of the city" and live in the "unclean tent."[1] That's not exactly the type of body-positive message I had hoped to receive from my Creator, nor do I know how to explain this to my daughter.

The text of Leviticus 15, for example, reads with terminology such as, "When a woman has a discharge, and the discharge in her body is blood, she shall be in her menstrual impurity for seven days, and whoever touches her shall be unclean until the evening. And *everything* on which she lies during her menstrual impurity shall be unclean. *Everything* also on which she sits shall be unclean. And whoever touches her bed shall wash his

---

1. Whitekettle, "Levitical thought."

clothes and bathe himself in water and be unclean until the evening."[2] Go ahead and try to feel good about yourself and your period after reading that passage. No wonder Cherie and I are still asking for tampons in secret at the age of thirty-seven; we have been conditioned to feel shame around the most common and normal act of our uteruses . . . menstruation. While the Old Testament serves an important purpose in telling the story of God's creation of and care for his people, I find many of the specific commands in books like Leviticus to be outdated and difficult to apply to my own life. When we as Christian women look to the Bible for understanding and insight around our bodies, we are met with limited and confusing ideas. We have not been encouraged as the body of Christ to foster creativity and imagination around our sexuality or reproductivity. In our exploration of our womb theology, I like to begin with the uterus: Why did God give me a uterus? Furthermore, in a body theology, why did God create my clitoris, vulva, menstrual cycle, vagina, and breasts? Inevitably, when answering these questions, we come to face many more questions, we will focus on this particular question for now: *why did God create women to bleed, and bleed monthly at that?* By definition the word *menstruation* translates in Greek to *mene* or moon, and in Latin, as *mensis* or month. The menstrual cycle quite closely approximates the month and the moon's 29.5-day synodic cycle. There are 3.8 billion women in the world, the vast majority of whom will experience menstrual bleeding throughout their lives. Of those billions of women, we *all* remember the story of the very first time we started to bleed.

Menarche: First Blood

The girls' bathroom adjacent to our sixth-grade classroom has two small metal cream-colored stalls. In a class of eighteen kids, we go in twos to the bathroom after recess ends. My childhood best friend, Sarah, is in the stall next to me, so she asks right away what happened when she hears me let out a small gasp. Blood. I had never seen blood in my underwear. She quickly retrieves Mrs. Napoli, our teacher, and we decide I should go home early. Because my mom is a single mom and is working forty minutes away, my aunt, or as everyone in my family calls her, "Nanny," comes to pick me up. If there was any woman created best for the job of the "period talk," it is my Nanny Janet. My Nanny is a soft, round-faced woman with shining eyes that are knowing and fiercely kind. She is a nurse who isn't afraid to

2. Leviticus 15:9–21 (NIV).

talk about anything: a woman's body, sex, orgasms, and she is definitely not afraid to talk about menstrual blood. Nanny takes me on a long drive and we stop at Mr. Burger to get a Coke with crushed ice (note that "Coke" in the South can mean any soda flavor). She is forthright and descriptive. She explains to me where the blood is coming from and what it means physiologically in my body. She assures me that this is a day of celebration, because I am becoming a woman, and my body is working perfectly and growing exactly as it should.

But even in her good care for me, my innocence was shaken that day; a childlike freedom evaporated and I became responsible and somewhat burdened with the new tasks to take care of my body. I was no longer able to practice and play sports without counting the weeks to determine which home or away games fell on my "time of the month." After my period began, I had to consider if I had a friend around who could check my shorts for leaks. I had to make note of things like what color pants I wore, and if I had a purse with enough space to carry feminine products. The carefree childhood was melding into the responsibilities of adolescence.

Menarche is the first menstruating blood in a girl's life and is to be celebrated as a rite of passage—the changing of a girl's body to a woman's body, signified through the shedding of blood.[3] My body indeed was starting to change, and for me it was the beginning of wrestling with the curse and blessing of bearing a woman's body. Although my Nanny Janet shared contextual information on the subject of menarche, it was not offered in spiritual connection and as part of God's design. As far as church goes, menstruation was not a topic my youth pastor's wife ever weighed in on, though I wish she had. There were youth group services where we separated guys from girls and talked about purity and the importance of wearing cover-ups over our swimsuits. Youth group never talked about God's design for making a woman's body in a particular way, to bleed so that women would be able to create life and offer the world the imagery of a Creator through our female organs. I never imagined cramping menstruation and pain in childbirth to be an invitation to understanding the suffering involved in creating and to know more about God. I could only conclude God had made women menstruate as part of the curse that we would know pain in childbirth, and our periods were possibly a chronic part of the curse, bleeding monthly to inhibit me from living in freedom. During adolescent years, my bleeding body was always there to annoy and embarrass me.

3. Wenham, *International Commentary*.

Something on Your Shorts

The day was going to be perfect. The sun was shining, and I was wearing new white cutoffs that looked great with my tan legs. It was the summer of my eighth-grade year, and our youth group outings were in full swing. A group of us were headed to spend the day tubing down the river. Most exciting of all, *he* was coming. Jared Ellingson. Yes, the tallest, cutest guy in my middle school would be there, all day, tubing with us. I was beside myself with nervous anticipation because Jared had called me every night this past week. I didn't know it then, but I spent most of my adolescent years in the dissonance of defining my body as either a holy being or a beautiful object when it came to romance and sexual attraction. Where I grew up, a good, Christian girl did not go swimming without shorts and a shirt to cover her swimsuit. So, I prided myself on being the perfect level of cute but not too revealing. I spent wasted hours over decisions such as which brightly colored tank top would accentuate my dark skin with my new white cutoffs. The limited, Christian mandate kept me oscillated in finding the perfect balance of alluring and modesty. Yet, the hormonal dance of adolescence did not disappoint, the day was magical, and the fun went on for hours: warm sun, flirtatious splashing from across the river, and laughter amongst friends. It seemed as if nothing could stain such a wonderful day. After the long ride home as we all climbed out of the fifteen-passenger van, my truest friend since third grade, Laurie, pulled me aside. She said the statement every adolescent girl never wants to hear: "Christy, there is something on your shorts." She walked dutifully behind me until we made it to her car and I carefully checked. There it was, in its obnoxious, unadulterated glory— blood. Yes, blood. I wrapped a towel around myself, mortified as we quickly said our good-byes. I wasn't supposed to start for another week, I thought! How long had the blood been there? Had Jared seen it? The hot feeling of shame crept through my body. My normal, good, and healthy-working body somehow made me feel less-than, embarrassed, ashamed, and impure.

Stigma. Shame. Taboo. These words are often associated with menstrual bleeding. From the oldest accounts of Scriptures, a woman was forced to leave her home when she bled. Can you imagine being sent out to the wilderness, to the space outside of your home? The very act of leaving your home holds an exile-like feeling, and with it an unconscious level of shame.

No matter where a girl grows up in the world, there's a very good chance that she will be inundated with endless myths and misconceptions about menstruation, as no bodily function—the exception of childbirth, perhaps—is more universally misrepresented and ubiquitously tabooed. From whence comes life, also comes our biggest source of shame. The cause of this stigma is truly perplexing. After thousands of years menstruating, humans should probably be over the sight of the blood itself, the odor, pain, and the waste it creates. And we certainly shouldn't be mystified by the nature of the act, as almost every mammal on the planet operates on a cycle, from the tiniest fruit bat to the great blue whale herself.[4]

Shame is defined, in particular for women, as the belief that one is debauched or unworthy, whereas guilt is derived from one's actions (e.g., what I have done is corrupt or dishonorable). Specifically, shame is identifying oneself as corrupt, depraved, or iniquitous separate from actions.[5] Consequently, ample research connects shame with feelings of unworthiness, subservience, and powerlessness.[6] Why is it that women feel shame or inconvenienced that their bodies bleed, when every female cycle requires blood?

Menstruation Research

Denial and desperation led me to search for understanding about my period and God's intent in having women bear this cyclical act of bleeding. In my research, I found that although the primary biblical perspectives on a woman's bleeding were a bit jarring, there were some threads of information that helped me understand these concepts more in depth. This next section will include theological references to issues of impurity and shame as they apply to female menstruation. As we will talk a lot about biblical tradition around menstrual cycles, it seems worthwhile to obtain a worldwide view.

4. Lockshin, *Women's Health*, 1.

5. Brown, "Shame Resilience Theory."

6. Brown, "Shame Resilience Theory"; Dearing and Tangney, *Shame in the Therapy Hour.*

The Biblical History of Bleeding

In Hebrew culture, *niddah* is a Hebrew word that describes a woman during menstruation. This period of time, usually twelve days, is not to be shared with a man, intercourse is not allowed, and the woman is regarded as impure. This imagery brings to mind the idea of bearing sin within our bodies, and the suffering it takes to return to purity. In addition, these twelve days were often closely connected to when a woman would ovulate, thus fertility was more likely to occur when adhering to these rules. In Jewish practices, a rabbi was to be consulted if there was any question whether a woman had finished *niddah,* or if she was having trouble conceiving a child. Women used small cloths to wipe the vagina for seven days after menstruation to see if any blood remained. Religiously, conservative/traditionalist members of the Orthodox Church observe the ancient practice of abstaining from Holy Communion during menstruation.[7]

When combating the idea of shame associated with blood, we must address the idea of "unclean/*tuma*" versus "clean/*tahor*" as it is referred to in the Old Testament. These two terms collectively are referred to in the book of Leviticus more than 200 times. When determining whether items to be used within worship and/or holy ceremonies are pure or impure, it is more accurate to associate "unclean" with common and "clean" with holy.[8] Clean or ritually pure is defined by the Hebrew word *tahor*, meaning the item is considered holy and able to be used in *acts of worship*. The word *unclean* in Hebrew is *tuma,* which translates more closely as "common," not the often-assumed idea of being "contaminated or dirty." Yet *tuma* can also be explained as more closely related to a "spiritual vacuum" or "spiritual death."[9] *Tuma* is what Adam and Eve brought into the world when they sinned, and it is considered a loss of spiritual power due to separation from God. Heather Farrell explains *tuma* this way:

> A man was also considered to be *tuma* after sexual intercourse because of the loss of potential life contained in each one of the sperm he spilled. In a similar way a woman was considered unclean after menstruation because each egg that she shed had the potential to become a new human life. Each egg inside a woman is filled with divine power, the power to activate and create human life. While the egg remains inside of her its spiritual potential

7. Lockshin, "Mikveh."

8. Farrell, "What Does It Mean?," 1–2.

9. Lockshin, "Mikveh."

is high. Yet once the egg passes through her body that spiritual potential leaves putting her in a state of *tuma*.[10]

This spiritual "energy of death" can only be cleansed and restored to purity through a ceremonial bath called *mikveh*. If you are familiar with Jewish culture, *mikveh*, a cleansing bath, is commonly taken around events such as weddings, before Yom Kippur, observing *niddah*, and other special events.[11] The cleansing bath has nothing to do with hygiene, as you must first wash yourself from head to toe before entering a cleansing bath; it is more like a baptism where you mark yourself as consecrated before God. *Tuma* and *mikveh* are also not particular to women, they are a part of all creation as it prepares itself to engage with holy and consecrated matters. For example, these cleansing baths are observed by Hasidic Jewish men every day or every Friday before Shabbat.[12]

Throughout the Old Testament God's people have been taught to communicate with their Creator through the resounding acts of sacrifice and worship. The greatest rituals of sacrifice and worship often involve life and death, and the *two greatest rituals of sacrifice and worship in the Bible are the birth and death of Christ*. In both of these events, there is a body broken to the point that blood and water are shed. When Christ's blood was shed on the cross, God the Father had to turn away because Jesus bore the sins of the world upon himself. Here, we also find the famous image of the *Madonna*, Mary, holding her son, the sacrificial Lamb, covered in blood. Joseph is not in this scene; it is Mary, the mother, whom God sent to comfort and hold Christ in his darkest hour. Christ's blood was the only acceptable sacrifice. The mother of Jesus is given the honor of comforting her broken and bleeding son's body. In sacrificial elements, blood has always been the powerful agent shed to cover or pay for something. Ritual maker and psychotherapist Heather Smith Stringer claims that within ritual, there is always worship, and worship involves: birth (awe) and death (sacrifice) and eventually rebirth (gratitude). Ritual orients to worship. The Madonna is holding death or releasing what has been emptied, i.e., menstruation is the ritual of a woman's body holding an egg and releasing it when it dies. An act of sacrifice is at the heart of worship. The hardest place to be, which is the point of letting go, is what is most necessary for new life to arrive. Our menstrual blood is symbolically a powerful offering to cover what is

10. Farrell, "What Does It Mean?," 1.
11. Lockshin, "Mikveh."
12. Huffington Post, "Religion."

impure, common, and unclean; to pay the price by being poured out of us, so that life can be reborn. As believers, God has given us two powerful elements: blood and water, which are symbols in times of sacrifice and worship. Jesus used these two elements often to display power: baptism, communion, and eternal life. Death's intent was to mock God when Jesus died on the cross, but Christ defeated death. We as Christ-followers no longer have to fear death or being unclean, for we are "washed in the blood of the Lamb" and "baptized in the Holy Spirit." Blood (life) and water (cleansing) are two elements of power we have as believers. For women, the theology of the womb highlights that menstruation and birth bear these two elements.

Cleansing Ritual

Mikveh is a cleansing ritual and also the specific ritual bath to purify and confirm that a woman has completed *niddah,* seven days without blood. This cleansing ritual, which is a huge part of how the biblical cultures interacted with a woman's period, often reminds me of the cleansing ritual around sacrificing an offering. If we think about the monthly cycle of a woman bearing *tuma,* bearing the absence of life, we must then consider the three remaining weeks when a woman bears *tahor* in her body, the potential of fullness and life. I enjoyed Rabbi Aryeh Kaplan's explanation of her understanding of *tuma* and the *mikvah.* She wrote:

> [W]ater represents the womb of Creation. When a person immerses in the mikvah, he is placing himself in the state of the world yet unborn, subjecting himself totally to G-d's creative power. In this context, it is easy to understand why immersion in a mikvah removes tuma. After the contact with death, we submerge ourselves in the substance from which life emerged.[13]

Immersion in a *mikveh* removes *tuma.* Immersion into the water removes death. Jesus on the cross immersed himself into death, into hell, and emerged into life—more so, eternal life. We know that this is what a baptism represents for people who come to faith, but I believe our menstrual cycles are invitations to immerse with Christ into a place of death so that we might bring forth fullness.

I did not grow up Jewish, nor can I imagine my pastor knowing when my period was occurring and weighing in on when I should have

---

13. Farrell, "What Does It Mean?," 2.

sex or the state of my fertility. The early church had laws and rules around women's menstrual cycles, and the present-day Catholic church informs couples through Natural Family Planning. Yet, in my Protestant church, there was very little taught or discussed of how God or the church could support women through their bleeding cycle and fertility. I don't necessarily think it is the church's place to engage with the physiological teaching of menstruation, but rather with the spiritual theology of it. I bring this up because I think we have long been too silent, and my faith desires to understand how spirituality fits with these secret places inside of me. I have been longing for community in this process. I want to understand how I can know God through my feminine body. God was not uncertain when he made a woman's body and her reproductive and sexual organs. If a woman is to know salvation through childbearing, I believe salvation is to also be studied and known through the understanding of the woman's womb and reproductive system. There are so many mysterious concepts about a womb and how it is formed in a woman. The theology of the womb has not begun to midrash over concepts such as the placental blood barrier, which keeps the maternal and fetal blood circulation systems completely separate. We must honor the mystery and brilliance of God by beckoning questions such as *why does an umbilical cord carry a mother's blood to nourish a baby who has her father's blood type* and *if blood type cannot cross the placenta, why can stress hormones affect the baby?*[14] Theologians have not begun to ask these questions of what God could be spiritually teaching us through the physiological realities in the makeup of the creation process.[15] Yet once again, I am getting ahead of myself. We must focus on understanding this one complex element, blood. Before we journey to the reproductive aspects of the womb, we must first study the bleeding of the womb. What do we do with a bleeding God? How do we come to understand a God who made women to bleed cyclically? As I studied the global history of menstruation I found that not only was our blood not meant to bring us shame, but we were never intended to navigate our bleeding alone.

Blood as Power

Our bleeding is an act of sacrifice, one that offers an invitation to understand the power and importance of creating and loving. I have been

14. Provençal and Binder, "The effects of early life stress."

15. Mölsä et al., "Functional role."

desperate to connect this internal belief with Christianity, but my research began by exploring the history of a woman's period outside of Scripture. Within the church, the woman's period had always been unaddressed or associated with cleansing rituals, not something to be engaged with by theologians from the pulpit. Mythology, psychology, and secular history considered menstruating women to be powerful; so powerful, in fact, that while menstruating, it is believed women hold a power strong enough to heal the sick or even possess increased psychic abilities.[16] Positive beliefs of sacredness and power associated with a woman's period are prevalent in some cultures.[17] In Cherokee culture, menstrual blood was a source of feminine strength and had the power to destroy enemies and stop catastrophic natural disasters. Interestingly, it was seen as especially dangerous to men's power to purify and destroy. One belief that brings me chills and intrigue is recognizing women's blood as a divine thing, particularly when it runs out of the body. This is the belief of old that the blood itself is "god spilling over."[18]

I am filled with wonder and fascination when I imagine my bleeding to be a divine act ordained by God; that when it runs out of my body, the blood itself is "the god spilling over." Wow, that sounds so much better than the shame I felt with the possibility of Jared seeing blood on my shorts. Yet, I want to contextualize these multicultural beliefs of bleeding as power within a Christian worldview, not simply a sociological view.

The concept of spilling over is connected to the research of Levitical law; Mesopotamian belief is that the womb is a wellspring.[19] Many cultures commonly used human parts of the body and the natural world in homological correspondence. Homology, or an acknowledged resemblance, indicates that the womb geographically and anatomically acts as a wellspring. Geographically, the wellspring was fed by the ocean, and when the wellspring was full it spilled over to feed the rivers. The analogy here coincides with the woman's womb as a body of water that continues to feed the earth with life-giving water. I imagine the ocean symbolizing God pouring out life-giving water to his "wellspring" vessels, female wombs, which spill over and bring life to the earth. There is a place in Scripture for a woman's bleeding to be seen as a wellspring of life spilling over.

16. Gumming, Gumming, and Kieren, "Menstrual mythology."
17. Tan, Haththotuwa, and Fraser, "Cultural aspects."
18. Whitekettle, "Levitical thought."
19. Whitekettle, "Levitical thought."

The overarching theme of this research conveys that female blood holds power. In Scripture, Christ's blood holds power. Why is Christ's blood shed on the cross so powerful? Why are we healed by the blood of the Lamb? We must look at the understanding of blood sacrifices. Most of us are familiar with the Old Testament understanding of covenants between God and his people. Covenants are made only in a ceremony with both sacrifices and vows. When God made a covenant, he would sacrifice, or shed, blood of animals on either side of an aisle; both parties were to walk through that aisle and thus a vow was solidified in covenant. Animal sacrifice was no longer needed after Christ became the ultimate sacrifice on the cross. Pay attention to how this ultimate sacrifice comes to us . . . through birth. Christ's birth is the next promise to be fulfilled, that a Savior will be born of a woman. So, we find ourselves at the scene of the manger where there are animals but no bloodshed, because this covenant involves human life. Where is the human bloodshed? Mary's womb. For a moment in the story, birth becomes the ceremonial act for God's promise to create and bring life to his people. It brings to mind the infamous curse in Genesis, that a woman will have pain in childbearing. Although this was a curse, I believe it was an invitation from God to women to participate in the act of covenant making and creating. I have begun to see birth and the menstrual cycle of a woman as a way of knowing God again after the separation of the fall. Think about the connection of intimacy we as women are invited into when we must endure pain within our own bodies to create life. The God we serve knows all too well the pain it requires to create eternal life; when he saved his children, it caused him pain. We as women are invited into that process in such an intimate way.

Life Blood Shed

The crucifixion is the most well-known act of bloodshed in theology and it brings forth the powerful gift of eternal life. As we mentioned, in the Old Testament the sacrifice of a lamb was a common ritual when making an oath between two people in a covenant. God in communion with his creation requires blood as part of an intimate promise. Christ on the cross was the bloodshed given for us, so his creation could commune with him forever in eternal life. There is no contesting that the precious blood of Jesus Christ on the cross saves us from eternal separation away from God. Christ's gift of ultimate love keeps us in communion with God, and we are not deemed to live this life alone. God made a covenant with us, a covenant sealed by the shedding of lifeblood. The promise of eternal communion was given in this act. When God created man and woman with the ability to procreate, God explains that we were never made to live in loneliness, but communally; creating life between a man and woman requires bloodshed. Women have been intimately invited into this ritual of remembrance in a very visceral way, through the monthly shedding of their own lifeblood. There is no human organ other than the womb that cyclically sheds blood. Culture and society have reduced the practice of menstruation to a nuisance, when in fact it is *an invitation from God to his creation to remember that lifeblood must be shed in order for life to be created.* I welcome you to the theology of *your* womb. May you never look at the shedding of your lifeblood the same way again. The Spirit is beckoning, can you hear? *Woman, you are fearfully and wonderfully made. You shed blood so that you can create life.*

Chapter 1 Questions: Why Do We Bleed?

1. Why do you think God created all women to bleed for the majority of their lifetimes?

2. Have you ever heard a sermon on the purpose of a woman's menstrual cycle? Why not?

3. Write out in 500 to 800 words the story of your first period.

4. How do you hope to talk to other women and your daughters about their periods?

2

Rites of Passage

In the red tent, the truth is known.
In the red tent, where days pass like a gentle stream,
as the gift of Innana courses through us,
cleansing the body of last month's death,
preparing the body to receive the new month's life,
women give thanks—for repose and restoration,
for the knowledge that life comes from between our legs,
and that life costs blood.

—Anita Diamant, *The Red Tent*

Alligator Hunting

L-O-S-E-R-ana. This nickname we had for where I grew up showed my true feelings as a teenager for my childhood home state. The long, sweltering hot days in the swamps of southwest Louisiana were spent hiking and blazing trails with four-wheelers through unmarked woods. At the age of thirteen, it was finally my turn to use the .22-rifle and kill my first alligator. After shooting it multiple times, my brother and I took the canoe in the lake and dragged out the five foot, three-inch-long, scaly beast. My rite of passage was hardly done by killing the creature; it would be truly tested as I attempted to tie the nerve-flinching creature down to our picnic table, then proceed to skin and later tan the hide of this gator. My main task, above avoiding nicks in the skinning, was to batter and fry the alligator meat to perfection for my family's dinner that night. Many people often ask what alligator meat tastes like, and truly, if battered and fried well, it tastes like a perfect blend of fish and chicken. One never wants to end up with chewy, overcooked fried gator bites.

This experience was one of the elite rites of passage that took place growing up as a Cajun girl in a town with a population of under 7,000 people. Most school holidays consisted of events such as the first day of squirrel hunting or quail hunting, and, if you were lucky, school let out early on the days we were going to a skeet shoot. There are rites of passage in everyone's life, although they may vary based on your ethnicity, social status, religion, and other factors. Rites of passage, ceremonies, and rituals are all historical ways in which women and men have engaged with their bodies as they grow older. Rites of passage are ways of marking an important stage in one's life or an event associated with crisis or change of status, especially birth, naming, puberty, marriage, illness, or death.[1] Adulthood is a social construct, and sociologists emphasize that marker events are a criterion for adulthood. Celebration and rites of passage amongst the women of my family feel familiar in other areas, but very limited when it comes to sacred feminine matters, particularly puberty. Periods and sex were not subjects the women in my family participated in corporately. I did not think highly about the privilege of becoming a woman and the responsibility of bearing a womb. Our best attempt at building a theology around our bodies was having my momma come to help and cook for me the two weeks after my kids were born. Other than that, no one really ever helped me make meaning of what was happening in my developing reproductive system. No one ever tied together how my feminine body displayed the glory of God and the reflection of a Creator. I didn't grow up spending my menstruation weeks in a spa retreat somewhere in the woods with my cousins and aunties. A repetitive weekend with my mothers of old, cooking all day long, is the closest experience I have to what it might have looked like to be handed down a ritual. In these women's kitchens, I found belonging through the collection of stories told while chopping vegetables and stirring continuously in black-iron pots. The theology I learned from my mothers of old, is that at the least, life is hard, and God never intended for us to do it alone.

1. Broderick and Blewitt, *The Life Span*.

Red Tent as Rite of Passage

On a global level, the most common lesson of beauty passed down from generation to generation, is mothers teaching their daughters to wash and tend to their hair. These practices of hygiene, along with women bathing in communal bath houses such as Turkish *hammam* or Finnish saunas, illustrate sisterhood. They transcend all cultures and become rituals particular to women and evidence that our ever-bearing, female bodies were made to live amongst tribes. Historical menstrual tents consisted of multiple generations of a selected tribe.[2] Women who were already experiencing menopause would join the menstrual tents to help the younger generations.[3] Women who were breastfeeding would bring their nursing babes along with their daughters. All females were welcome in the week of bleeding. The time was filled with spa-like and grooming activities such as bathing, massage, hairdressing, storytelling, and dream sharing. In days of old, this ritual journey was done with your great-grandmother, grandmother, mother, aunts, sisters, cousins, and daughters. The unknowns of a woman's body were illuminated in the vast differences and similarities of the bodies in one's family and tribe; each body reflecting back to you that you come from one another and are connected to each other in a mysterious way. We need our tribes; our tribes reflect and remind our bodies both of who we are and that we are not alone.

Even today, we need to have consistent gatherings amongst women so that we can feel less alone in our own female bodies. This historical act of sharing in a communal initiation to a girl's menstruation has long been practiced throughout the world. Global historic rituals of girls' first blood are overall culturally seen as negative, *except* for places where the ritual is done in community. For instance, in India, Hindu women tend to view menstruation, especially first menstruation or menarche, as a positive aspect of a girl's life. In South India, girls who experience their menstrual period for the first time are given presents and celebrations to mark this special occasion. Ancient Hebrew women took their girls out into the wilderness to dig a hole to bury their first blood and let it replenish the earth, while young girls in Ghana sit under ceremonial umbrellas and people brings gifts and pay homage.[4] There are even positive accounts from male

2. Abber and Abi-Najeme, "Around the World."

3. Diamant, *The Red Tent.*

4. Gottlieb, "Sex, Fertility and Menstruation."

religious leaders in the Ivory Coast, who describe menstruation as "the flower of a tree which needs to flower before it can bear fruit."[5] These other viewpoints contradict the imposed "ideology of sin, dirt, pollution" that has been given to menstruation.[6] Within the cultures that believed menstruation was a positive thing and something to be done in community, the women spoke of their time of menstruation, postpartum, nursing, and menopause in community as positive. The red tent concept is a universal and important part of caring for a woman's body through her womb's entire life cycle. Lastly, it was a Ulithi woman of the South Pacific who explained her culture's understanding of the red tent, where breastfeeding women join menstruating women in huts along with their children. Although it is stunning to me that this is happening in the present day, she explains that the tents have a "kind of a party atmosphere."[7]

The day I started my first period, my Nanny took me to get a Coke at a fast-food joint. There was no party, no flowers, no umbrellas or dances, and definitely no digging holes in the ground. In fact, in southern Louisiana, my family was considered to be very progressive because we actually spoke about periods and sex. I came from a "good, Christian home" and went to private school, so there was no sex education for me. Had I been born in Eastern Africa, every female in the village would have attended my coming of age celebration and their gift would have been showing me, by dance, three sexual positions that enhance female pleasure during sex. This is a very common practice in Africa, as women believe sexual pleasure is important knowledge that must be passed down to the next generation. My experience of getting the sex talk from my parents was very different. One Sunday night after church, my mom took my younger sister and me to Ryan's Steakhouse buffet and told us about sex. I will never forget how she illustrated sex with a yellow and green gummy bear from our dessert plate, and to this day I struggle to eat yellow and green gummy bears without thinking about that horrifically embarrassing conversation. Often for Western Christian women, these conversations about periods and sex are not easily passed down. Even during times where only women are present, there is silence around these subjects, which leads us to interpret that we must never speak of them but somehow figure them out on our own.

5. Lee and Sasser-Coen, "Memories of menarche."
6. Brink, "Some Cultures."
7. Gottlieb, "Sex, Fertility and Menstruation."

Rites of passage look different in every culture and community. Research shows us the importance of development, regulation, and resilience through marking significant events in our lives.[8] These acts or rituals teach our minds the importance of marking our moments of celebration and grief.[9] Martin Prechtel's words beckon me to continue to mark my life events through ceremonies and rituals: "Rites-of-passage ceremonies are not just for young people to pass into adulthood. *Life change rituals should accompany every stage of life* and anticipate the people's full expression of grief."[10] The word *grief* stands out to me. Do rites of passage and a woman's coming of age, such as a menstrual cycle or birthing, express grief? *Aging at its core teaches us that for something to live, something must die.* When I began the study of women's wombs and the rites of passage around the process of menstruation and birth, I never anticipated the invitation to grief. The grief I have found that one must bear for something new to become alive is a bit overwhelming. These concepts, of celebration and grief through the ritual of a woman's menstrual cycle, continuously ask our bodies to engage the spiritual significance of creating.

At the Least, Not Alone

My baby sister's tears look out of place against the beautiful, Belizean ocean background. We are standing on the dock with our scuba gear waiting to load the boat for a beginner diving class. Her small, tan, twelve-year-old frame is shaking in the wind and her tears seem to be more about pain than embarrassment. It was her first time having to wear a tampon because, as we all know at an innate level, period pads are not best suited for water activities. Even though I was comfortable with my knowledge about periods at the age of fourteen, I didn't know for sure whether there was some universal unspoken rule that you never go swimming in the ocean while on your period, or if it was an old wives' tale. But who could I ask? Our male, Rastafarian diving instructor did not look like he would know. Although we never disclosed it out loud until years later, my little sister and I both feared at a primal level that sharks and barracudas would be drawn to her bleeding body, and we might meet our demise that day. My parents had been divorced over six years now and we were on an island with only

8. Fosha, Siegel, and Solomon, eds., *The Healing Power.*

9. Siegel and Solomon, eds., *Healing Trauma.*

10. Prechtel, *The Smell of Rain on Dust.*

my dad as our caregiver. Sending an email to my mom and getting a timely response before the underwater excursion was out of the question. Anyone could see my sister was in pain; the long boat ride and dive had required her to use a super-sized tampon. I felt helpless as an older sister with such limited knowledge about tampon sizes, but I focused on my sister's comfort regardless of my ignorance. All I could do was stand next to her, offering the assurance that we would be in this together. I myself had my own nightmare experiences early on with tampons, one in particular in which my mom had to come in the bathroom and help remove the tampon, which I had inserted into the wrong hole. Needless to say, my empathy for painful tampon insertions was at high awareness. It was a long day on the barrier reef, and I was vigilantly aware of the sea creatures around us, making note of how far my little sister was from me and if I could see blood anywhere in the clear blue water. I was not going to leave her side, even if it meant we died together under shark attack.

We survived that excruciating day, but all in all, at age fourteen or forty, periods were no friend of mine, nor any of the women I knew. In some cases, as a teenager without full knowledge and left to my own imagination, bleeding seemed life-threatening. Periods were not only a nuisance and embarrassing; they were painful, and possibly the ultimate curse on all women. Since that fearful day diving with my sister, I have had my period over one hundred times and learned a lot about the physiological aspects of menstruating, but I continue to wrestle with the idea of bleeding alone.

Bleeding Together

Often on dark winter nights in Seattle, a group text will emerge, beckoning all the women in my community to meet at the spa. Ladywell Spa is a small, women-only spa and sauna near my house. My tribe and I find ourselves slipping away from our husbands and sleeping kids into the moonlit night to gather for hours of bathing, talking, massages, reading, and resting. Our bodies feel at home being together. In my ever naïve and Hollywood imagination, I believe there would have been a similar feel to this in the menstrual tent, outside the city in the wilderness during the days of old. At the spa, the salt and charcoal rooms are heavy with heat, drawing perspiration from our exhausted bodies, and there is a sense of detoxing what our exhaustion has cost us. The circuit of cold, warm, and hot pools are indeed where cleansing takes place, much like a *mikveh* bath, removing what has died. The hormonal imbalances and stresses of the womb cycle are met with the conversations and self-care of other women who know what it means to have their bodies bleed. The aging bodies of other women teach us and call us into the invitation of our own journey with our aging body. It is in the sharing of these cycles that we learn who we are, where we have come from, and, eventually, where we will go.

Some groups of women say that their periods sync up when they live in the same house together. Although there is inconclusive evidence that the menstrual cycles of women living together sync up, it was true for the house of six girls I lived with in college. It seems to have been a reality for those who lived in the red tent. Women have been gathered together in a menstrual tent for centuries prior, engaging in collective self-care rituals through their menstrual cycle. Yet in cultures which do not participate in this historical act, we must ask ourselves what bleeding with one's tribe looks like now that we live with so much space between us.

Separate but Communal

The loud, scratchy, white paper I sit on covers the examination chair in my OBGYN's office. I have a thin, cotton, terribly-patterned smock barely covering me. There is little dignity left after a birth and six weeks of postpartum which have consisted of bleeding, not sleeping, nursing, and pure exhaustion. It has been forty-two days since I birthed my little one, and while he is in the other room getting circumcised, I am having a pelvic exam to clear me for sexual activity. Truly, these two once highly spiritual acts have been reduced to an office visit, insurance, and mostly paperwork. There is no drum beating or ritual dance around my son's circumcision; there is no ceremony at all. My husband holds a bubble gum liquid-covered pacifier in his mouth while the circumcision procedure is done. In the room across the hall, my ceremony is even less exciting. I am alone, shivering in my thin paper drape with my saggy, exhausted body, waiting for the doctor. I can hear my sweet baby boy screaming in agony. It is my turn. My doctor's purple gloves go on, the familiar stirrups are routine, and the pelvic exam is quick. It is all so strange to me, the sterile and cold process our medical systems have implemented for women recovering from giving birth. It makes complete sense to allow our bodies to rest after bleeding and birthing, but the loneliness we experience in the process is taxing. There is no red tent in the wilderness for me to retreat to, no spa-like baths to soak in and heal.

There are no women from my family streaming through the rooms, little girls getting their hair braided, no other moms breastfeeding their young, there are no grandmothers holding babies on their laps so the mommas can sleep. It occurs to me that for the past forty weeks of my pregnancy, I have had regular check-ups, monthly then weekly, and now this will be the last one and my body will be left to return to normal activities, and in turn my body will trade places with my sweet baby who will be the one who receives the routine care. Other than my annual health exam, it won't be until I am pregnant again that I will visit this doctor.

Fortunately, there was no vaginal tearing during this birth, so I receive a slight praise of my recovery speed, and then I am free to go. How I wish I had spent the past forty days with women who loved and doted on me and my baby. If only instead of this last doctor's visit, I was driving home from a spa retreat in the mountains having spent weeks with my closest girlfriends getting hair-conditioning treatments and pedicures. My postpartum spa fantasy is not too far from plausible in an Eastern culture, and luckily, my closest friends are doulas, midwives, and even a lactation consultant. Should I have spent weeks in a mountain retreat with a sisterhood holding my child and helping me get sleep and breastfeed, I would have possibly been rejuvenated to return home to my husband and older kids; to step back into the throes of family life. A woman can dream, can't she? What if Levitical law was singling out these allotted days away from men for a woman's body to recuperate, not simply because of impurity reasons? Maybe God knew the recovery time it takes for a woman's body after bearing a child. Maybe time away is what a woman's soul needs to birth, bleed well, and then heal and return well. One might dream that a woman's time of completion would be a bit more communal and more celebratory. I ask my doctor about these ideas I'm musing on, and she informs me that although a woman's vagina is cleared for sexual activity after six weeks postpartum, she explains that a woman's body needs two years to fully heal from a pregnancy.

I can't really share much with my husband in understanding or exploration during my period, but my girlfriends and I carry a similar responsibility within our bodies. It isn't uncommon for me to ask my husband to pick up tampons or pads for me at the grocery store. My husband and I share an app on our phones that gives him a reminder when my period is coming and when to expect PMS symptoms. In so many ways, I am very removed from the biblical practices of menstruation, from those followed by all the women before me and currently by many women in other cultures.

Originally, each cycle invited every woman into a time where she would gather with all the other women and live communally with them. PMS, bloating, cramps, heating pads, warm tea, massages, and Epsom salt baths were abundant; and this was all done together as a community of women. Ancient traditions around separation time during periods were filled with a week of preserving the female culture. This culture was one where older women held newborns while young women listened to their mothers tell stories upon stories. It would have been similar to a week-long slumber party filled with conversation, cooking, wine, manicures and pedicures, haircutting, and eyebrow tweezing. If such an idea inspires you, let's consider why we have drifted away from this practice and how society now engages women's menstrual cycles and post-postpartum. How can we as a church body of women engage our bodies and this invitation in a new way?

Church in the Red Tent

My friend Marge is sitting on the couch in the beautiful great room at our church's annual women's retreat. I was planning on going back to bed. The house is still, and mornings are often guarded, quiet, and slow so that mommas can get caught up on their years of not sleeping in. It is early enough that it wouldn't be a big deal to pee and head back for another hour of sleep, but her silver hair and quiet demeanor draw me to the fire near her, so I ask sweet Marge why she is up so early. She calmly tells me in this stage of menopause she has insomnia often and has spent the dark hours of the night praying and meditating. Marge is one of the only women in her fifties who made it to the retreat this weekend and it seems brave of her to situate herself with others in such different stages of life. As I rest my pregnant belly down into the couch next to her, she tells me of her experience moving through the stages of menopause. We talk for a while until our conversation is interrupted by the familiar, rhythmic-sucking sound of a breast pump. A young momma who is spending her first nights away from her baby is watching home videos on her phone and filling up breast milk bags to freeze. Another group of ladies has gathered near the coffee pot and I turn to see friends rubbing each other's backs and asking how their sleep was.

The idea of meeting together, a huge group of women, of all ages, sounds chaotic and wonderful in the same breath. The imagery of the red tent comes to mind; the idea of tribes of women, all ages, all phases of life, gathering together monthly in the wilderness whether or not there is bleeding. Infants, prepubescent girls, menstruating, pregnant, postpartum, menopausal females all gather, because there is a place for each of them, a job if you will, that they are needed in the "tent" to contribute to the gender of women continuing in a holistic way. There are storytellers, story-bearers, those who give touch, those who receive touch, those who hold babies, rock babies, burp babies for the mommas who haven't slept for nights upon nights. Each woman plays a role in holding up other women in whatever stage they are in; and at each stage you are in it is imperative to contribute to someone else making it through the stage they are in.

I have known throughout my entire life that women plan their major life events around their bleeding. I know women who have scheduled their dates, their sporting events, and especially their weddings around their menstrual cycles. Women plan around their bleeding and usually it is seen as a nuisance. Women of old had it down, the great-grandmothers listened to their bodies and gathered together and formed a place where the sisterhood bled together. With curiosity about their gender and their purpose, these gathered women respected their bleeding bodies, bled well, and were replenished. Thus, the concept of the red tent was formed, a place where women would congregate outside of the encampment.

Sancta in the Wilderness

Historically, the red tent was not merely set up outside of the tribes of Israel's encampment, rather the sojourn to the red tent was described as being sent into the wilderness. To get the full context of why women were sent so far away when they were bleeding, we must revisit the understanding of Biblical laws of being unclean or impure. The Levitical law of purity was interested in the genital discharge of males and females, not blood. What this means is that impurity was not ascribed to the female body in general or to discharge from sexual arousal. While one might find this information a bit over-explicit, this is an important distinction, as the Levitical law is often taken out of context and impurity is assigned to women's bodies and sexuality as a whole. To further explain this idea, a menstruating woman was impure for her duration of menstrual discharge, which could vary from three to nine days. A postpartum woman's discharge could vary from twenty to sixty days, during which she was considered impure. The Levitical rule of thumb averaged separation for seven days for one's menstrual cycle and forty days for a woman's postpartum. A woman wasn't considered pure again until menstrual or puerperal discharge returned.[11] Note the number of days specified, seven or forty, are both biblical numbers representing completion.

The reason impurity and purity mattered in Levitical law was attributed to the understanding of *sancta*, the divine realm where Yahweh dwelled, which was located at the center of Israel's wilderness camp. As noted throughout Leviticus and Numbers, the belief was that when a woman was bleeding, she was a threat to *sancta* and must move to the wilderness beyond the encampment.[12] In the Old Testament, the Israelites set up tents in a circular pattern, similar to any ancient ritual circle. The center held the tribe's most important possessions, the tabernacle, and the outer periphery was a further circle of safety or space protecting the center where the tabernacle inhabited *sancta*. A normal layout would include: the center tabernacle, the circle of the sons of Levi around the sancta, and the outer circle of the remaining of the twelve tribes.[13] Imagine women being sent outside of this camp arrangement and its safety into the wilderness whenever they were bleeding. If we are left to the vague and harsh concept of the Old Testament's demand to extricate bleeding women into the wilderness, we miss the wonder of the wilderness and the Old Testament's promise and celebration of a woman's bleeding. In our personal endeavors to educate ourselves, many women in the church have stepped out and owned the stories within their bodies. The idea of separation from men is a harsh idea, until you realize it was because women's blood was seen as powerful and both a threat to men and to the *sancta* of Yahweh.

Separation was actually done communally. Women would retreat *together* during these seasons of separation from their home. Because there is sparse education on the ideas of red tent living, we must use our imaginations to understand God's intention of women bleeding in community. For it is in this communal rite of passage within the red tent that one learns how to sing the song of the womb.

11. Diamant, *The Red Tent.*
12. See Appendix A.
13. See Appendix C.

Chapter 2 Questions: Rites of Passage

1. What rites of passage stand out in your personal life? How has culture impacted these practices for you?

2. How is your menstrual cycle engaged in your family system?

3. There isn't a week that goes by in my therapy practice that female clients don't come to seek help in alleviating the discomfort and embarrassment they feel being Christian women who are trying to engage their sexual and reproductive health. These journeys are usually done alone and in silence, all while combating shame-filled lies. God is telling us so much through our female bodies, and we each have a deep invitation to God's goodness and our own goodness when we understand how we are made. Do you consider your sexuality healthy?

4. How have you come to understand the idea of the red tent? Do you have a group of women, a sisterhood, that you can connect with around your body and God's design of your body?

5. The book *Taking Charge of Your Fertility* by Toni Weschler is a vital tool to help women understand the cycle of their reproductive system. Sadly, few women even know much about their physical reproductive organs or their uses. Why does this matter? Ask yourself, if I don't know about my body on a physiological level, how can I begin to understand it on a spiritual and psychological level?

3

A Singing, Storytelling God

We use all our senses to wring the truth from things,
to extract nourishment from ideas, to see what there is to see,
know what there is to know, to be the keepers of the creative fire,
and to have intimate knowing about the Life/Death/Life Cycles of all nature
—this is an initiated woman.

—CLARISSA PINKOLA ESTES[1]

Learning to Ululate

THE SWEAT RUNNING DOWN my inner thighs could not begin to convey the intense heat we were experiencing in the remote desert of this small Southern Kenyan region. Our group's van had driven through two hours of desolate and monochromatic deserts of beige, occasionally passing a gunman-guarded well or some desert animals crossing the sandy road. When we stopped there were no huts in sight, only one large tree with almost 200 brilliantly adorned women and children dancing and singing around it. The stark image of women and children clothed in bright, rainbow-colored material contrasted against their smooth ebony-polished skin. In the middle of this desert, under the shade of what seemed to be a tree of life, this most royal congregation gathered. As we were welcomed by this tribe,

1. Estés, *Women Who Run with the Wolves*.

30

the women's intricately rainbow-beaded necklaces bowed like canopies around their necks and covered their shoulders. The exquisite multicolored necklaces were more mesmerizing than a large diamond ring on a woman's finger. I couldn't take my eyes off the beadwork or, like a typical American, wonder where I might purchase such jewelry for myself. I would come to learn that these necklaces were what we would consider an engagement ring, signifying the women who wore them were married.

After we distributed water and food supplies, they in turn shared their own gift, one that I will take to my grave. In an awe-inspiring rite of passage, the women began to sing, moan, and ululate. The large rainbow-colored beads began to rock back and forth around their long slender necks, sounding much like a music shaker. Their neck movements accelerated and began to move in the most awkward jerks, yet they smiled the most beautiful smiles. Like one tapping their leg while listening to a favorite song, I couldn't help but attempt unsuccessfully to move my neck in this motion. It was then that the sound emerged and they began to ululate, a sacred practice of honor and emotion; a sound of celebration or remorse. Their necklaces vibrated much like I believed their uvulas did, moving back and forth to produce that sound. I did not then know the word was *ululation*, and to be honest, the first time I looked I reread the definition describing the movement of tongues and uvulas. I quickly checked Wikipedia to make sure *uvulas* were uvulas and *not* vulvas, because that would be an awkward mix-up. These women, in the middle of a vacant and dusty field in Nairobi, were flawlessly mentoring me, honoring me, and teaching me by offering me the gift of an ululation, which humans, and more often women in particular, curate. There was such an indistinguishable power in their voices; an almost mesmerizing strength that awed me.

This would not be the only time I heard ululation during my weeks there. I later attended a funeral of a small child who died of AIDS, and at his funeral there was this same type of ululating, a similar jerking of the neck, shaking of the beads—but this ululating had a gurgling-like, wailing sound of deep grief. The imagery of Psalms 126 comes to mind when I think about the practice of ululating: "Our mouths they were filled, filled with laughter. Our tongues they were loosed, loosed with joy. Those who go out weeping, carrying seed to sow, will return with songs of joy, carrying sheaves with them."

History of Ululation

Ululation is not limited to African culture. It is actually a worldwide practice. An ululation is a long, wavering, high-pitched vocal sound using the
tongue and uvula, resembling a howl. It is used to express strong emotion
such as cheering, mourning, and honoring someone. It is sometimes used
as a battle cry, a wailing accompanying deep grief, or celebration welcom-
ing a bride, groom, or both.[2] Ululating is often also done in spiritual ceremonies such as at a *hachnasat sefer Torah*, the dedication of Torah scrolls,
and during circumcisions, communal celebrations, and communal burials.
Although ululation sounds similar across most people groups, I came to
find the practice of raising one's voice aloud is most common at ceremonies
or rituals during rites of passage. All humans raise their voices, making a
sound resembling the strongest of emotion, during times of both celebration and mourning.[3] In researching and experiencing other cultures as
they mentored me in my own attempts to learn to ululate, I found that the
practice of using one's voice to express emotion is universal in all tribes and
people groups. Ululating is a practice we find in South and Central Asia,
Serbia and Cyprus, Spain, the Middle East, Africa, and many parts of South
America.[4] Within the Western culture it is less common, and I welcome
you to listen to my own ululation throughout this book, and furthermore,
I invite you to create your own. Begin by listening for others around you
who are ululating, making a sound with their voices that holds conviction
of grief or celebration. Ultimately, if you listen to others you will begin to
recognize your own, yes, your ululations. These are the sounds you hear
yourself make when you are deeply moved by something in your story. For
you have been singing, howling, ululating for a long time. You, woman,
have a loud song that erupts in delight and horror. If you have silenced this
place, I invite you to listen. You will hear your own sounds coming from
your own tongue, these holy ululations longing to be unleashed.

Story Keepers and Storytellers

Women are often storytellers by nature; mothers, story keepers. As the
primary caregiver in an infant's life, a mother holds all the memories of

2. Janus, "Laughter and the Limits of Identity."
3. Jacobs, "Ululation in Levantine Society."
4. Ezeh, "Sex, custom and population."

a child's story before they have the capacity to remember their own story. In the Bible, men's lineage is often accounted through their bloodline; our mothers' lineage was passed down through stories told amongst other women who gathered in the red tent. Stories of where we come from are highly vital to the well-being and future of a person. *To know who we are and where we are going, we often need to be reminded of where we came from.* While men often have a stronger sense of where they come from, as their family name is passed down from generations prior, women often struggle with identity due to a lack of legacy.

In my work with women over the past decade, it is narrative therapy and story work that has most resonated in the therapy room. Female clients in my office have used the following words to describe their mental health: "a withered psyche," "a fatigued soul," "an exhausted mind," "an emptied womb," or "a silenced voice." Whether through stories of domestic violence, spiritual silencing, sexual shame, or self-esteem issues, women have forgotten where they come from; in some cases, they were never told. The Bible is limited in its stories of women, which leaves many Christian women starving for direction and theology to fit their understanding. We must learn to tell our stories well, and we often learn them from the stories of the mothers before us. Author Anita Diamant explains the biblical experience of the red tent and the symbolism it held for generations of women:

> But the other reason women wanted daughters was to keep their memories alive. Sons did not hear their mothers' stories after weaning. In the ruddy shade of the red tent, the menstrual tent, they ran their fingers through my curls, repeating the escapades of their youths, the sagas of their childbirths. Their stories were like offerings of hope and strength poured out before the Queen of Heaven, only these gifts were not of any god or goddess—but for me. I can still feel how my mothers loved me. I have cherished their love always. It sustained me. It kept me alive. Even after I left them, and even now so long after their deaths, I am comforted by their memory.[5]

Storytelling passes down concepts about how to understand life. In my practice, many women have forgotten their own stories and thus don't know how to speak for themselves; they don't recognize their own voice or remember the song of the womb. Famous storytellers Gertrud Mueller Nelson and Clarissa Pinkola Estés are psychologically trained and teach

5. Diamant, *The Red Tent,* 3.

healing of the feminine. Their work reminds the feminine soul that it must be free. Nelson tells stories to all wounded women, offering healing through the act of dwelling free.[6] Estés explains that the process of domesticating a woman can injure or dry up her soul.[7] Domestication, by definition, is to be under the rule of someone other than oneself. Both scholars speak to the effects of the feminine soul being injured by enslavement. To be freed and to bring life back to our wounded selves, we must remember the song from our womb, and sing to our dried-up bones.

Dried Bones Stories

I want to share two stories: the first is the valley of dried bones, the biblical account in Ezekiel, where God asks him to bring dry bones to life; the second is the mythical story of La Hueresa, the bone woman, who rebirths dead bones.

In the first story, from Ezekiel,[8] we are captivated by the life-giving power of God. The vision begins with Ezekiel explaining that the Spirit of the Lord showed him cracked and dried bones scattered across a desolate valley. God commands and gives Ezekiel the power to speak words of life, words that would bring back tendons and flesh to these bones. The bones rattle and come to life—a whole people group revived from death.

In the old Mexican tale of La Huesera,[9] the bone woman, a young wife dies under the hand of an abusive husband after she can give him no children. Her bones are gathered by an elderly woman whose work is to gather the lost, scattered, and dried bones and bring them back to life. She sings a song over the dried bones until flesh comes back and the woman is again alive. The woman is given a new name and a fruitful life.

In both of these stories: *voice, song, soul, and most importantly, the Spirit of the Lord* (the Creator) brought life back to the bones and they lived again. Specifically, in Scriptures we know the dried bones are signifying lost hope: "Our bones are dried up and our hope is gone . . ." (Ezekiel 37:11). In verse 14, the Lord goes on to say, "I will put my Spirit in you and you will live. Then you will know that I the Lord have *spoken*, and I have done it, declares the Lord." We see this theme the story of La Huesera. The woman had

6. Sellers, "Vow of Onah."
7. Estés, *Women Who Run with the Wolves*.
8. Ezekiel 37.
9. Tippett, "Soul, Food, Sex and Space."

died of hopelessness from not being able to bear children for her husband. She was brought back to life by a life song being sung over her. These stories resonate with what I see every day in my therapy practice. Humans that have been stolen from by trauma and abuse are being brought back to life through stories and songs of freedom. There is something holy about the Spirit of God breathing life back into a place of hopelessness and dried-up bones. Women are invited to be more involved in the re-birthing process by understanding the story God put inside of them, particularly through the womb. A life song dwells inside of every womb. In these intimate invitations to co-create life with our Maker, we have very little physical control over the creation of a human soul. Yet, research implores that the mother's voice, health, and psyche are impactful in the process of co-creation.

Whether it is in the act of speaking, singing, or ululating, we are all invited to co-create life. Proverbs affirms that "The tongue has the power of life and death."[10] The voice of a female, in particular, is generationally a sounding board of stability in many cultures. Across this school of thought, a woman's song or voice is realized through her intuition or gut instincts. Each woman bears a different sound, which is accessed through her own knowing of her *inner self*. I believe this is why evil has committed itself to the silencing of women, both their voices and their bodies. One pathway to healing is to learn the songs within us, the song of our womb.

The Song of the Womb

You, woman, have a loud song that erupts when you experience delight or horror. If you have silenced this place, I invite you to listen. You will hear your own sounds coming from your own story. Ululating has captured me most in grief, and it is commonly found in the prayers that bring life back from death. This is where I stumbled upon the song within my womb—it began by my knowing where I come from.

In many passages in the Bible it is common to find the genealogy history listed by males, such as, "and Boaz begat Obed, and Obed begat Ishai" or "the genealogy of Judah unto Jesse, the father of David." As women, we have been looking to a text written by men, to men. The Bible offers us a clear lineage of males, which I think is an incredible gift for men to know their birthright. But what of a woman who is also given a birthright at birth? A birthright is defined as a natural or mortal right possessed by

10. Proverbs 18:21.

everyone; *jus soli* or *jus sanguinis*, the standard birthrights for citizenship to a nation.[11] *We all come from a lineage of priestesses, prophetesses, and queens, and our birthright is to live into our voice and story.* Women have birthed nations from their wombs without knowing their own citizenship in the kingdom of God, thus we must know our own birthright in order to teach our children their birthrights. Often when I invite clients to explore their birthright, I ask them to begin by telling me the nation of wombs from which they came. For example, my birthright is:

> I, Christy Angelle Védrine, am from the womb of priestess Mary Christine Jakovich, daughter of prophetess Rosemarie Mollica, granddaughter of queen Dora Rose Brocato, great-granddaughter of prophetess Dora Ellen Campaña.

This is the beginning of my knowing my birthright, and when I can name what rights I possess from birth, I begin to listen to the song of the wombs I came from. Thus, I am invited to understand the song my womb is beginning to sing, the song I sing for sinew and flesh to come back alive on dried-out bones. If the first step to knowing oneself is to learn your story, then the road map begins by seeking where you came from. The ultimate goal of living into one's story is to learn how to sing about story through your life song. To bear the image of God is to sing the song of our story. For women, this song is often found in our wombs, a deep belly song we are invited to sing. This is the song of the womb. The lyrics are found in the womb from which we were born and the womb from which you create. This ever-bearing legacy we create will continue long after we are gone. The cadence comes from the hum as our vocal chords dance when we each sing from our own womb, our particular story. No two wombs sound exactly alike.

Rocking Chairs and Humming

Tucked in the corner of my momma's upstairs bedroom, there is a 1970s print upholstered rocking chair that I was practically raised in. Over the two decades spanning my mom's child-rearing years, my siblings and I have left scratches and marks on the wooden armrests. We each carved deep grooves during our collective hours being rocked and sung to while in my momma's arms. My secure attachment to my mom was formed and

11. Farson, *Birthrights*, xii, 21.

most influenced in that rocking chair. Upon sitting in this same chair as an adult child holding my own baby, I am instantly taken by the methodical creaking, which almost echoes a childhood rhythmic tune. I can remember countless hours of my mom rocking me in this chair and singing hymns to me until I fell asleep. My mom taught me two things inherently since birth: how to rock and how to hum. There are a few things that are proven in bio-psychological research to help aid the hippocampus and calm the limbic system: essential oils, *rocking*, tapping or swaying, and singing or *humming*. Post-traumatic stress happens in the limbic system. We know the amygdala turns *on* the stress response and the hippocampus turns *off* the stress response in the brain. In my birthing story, when my firstborn child was stillborn at forty-one weeks, my postpartum was filled with annihilating PTSD. I could not sleep, all I could do was sit in the rocking chair and weep.

During the days after I lost my son Brave, I would pull this rocking chair as close to the window as possible and let the sun pour over me as I wept and wailed. It was the action that I inherently knew as a way to comfort, and rocking was a body memory I longed to be doing with my newborn son. Because I had buried my sweet baby boy just days earlier, I rocked the wailing, inner child in me. I cradled her exhausted, bleeding body in that wooden rocking chair. I wept and rocked for weeks.

As the weeping began to lessen, I would try to sing as a way of comfort. Yet, every time even the simplest lyric would form on my lips, I would begin weeping again. I actually did not sing a worship song for a little over a year after Brave died. The months of my pregnancy with him growing within me were often filled with song, a few songs that I don't know if I will ever sing aloud again. Worship has always been such an emotional and vulnerable place for me since losing him. When death muted my songs for a long time, I learned to hum.

Humming has long history. The poet Nikki Giovanni talks about how it must have been a woman who hummed the first negro spiritual. She says only a woman, who did not know all the languages of those locked in bows of the passenger slave ships, could have known to settle her people by humming. If you have never heard the hum of a dark-skinned matriarch who is settling her people down, close your eyes and imagine it. A woman, who has birthed and raised her own children, had them stripped from her by death or slavery, can still ground all fears with the resonating buzz and deep hum from her vocal cords. Can you hear it? Humming is the song of Mother God. This sound of God is deep, melodious, and holy. It can calm a crying child, attune with post-traumatic stress, accompany the abandoned soul, and settle the devastated orphan. Only after burying my son did I begin to learn about the theology of suffering, how our humming, ululating, and rocking can soothe the grieving and anxious soul.

When loss is the loudest thing we hear, we must learn our song again, and louder that before. Often it is not comprised of words, but rather a deeply resonating hum.

Chapter 3 Questions: A Singing, Storytelling God

1. Once you are in a quiet, worshipful place, try to hum as a prayer to minister to your heart or sing over yourself as one who is calling life from places that have died within you.

2. What do you think is the sound of your womb's song?

Song of the Womb Exercise:

In researching and experiencing other cultures as they mentored me in my ululations, I came to find they are in all people, the sounds resembling the strongest of emotion, used in joy and celebration, and mourning and grief. I invite you to begin listening to others around you who are ululating and ultimately, I long for you to listen for your own ululations. For you have been howling for a long time. You, woman, have a loud song that erupts in delight and horror. If you have silenced this place, I invite you to listen, you will hear your own sounds coming from your own tongue. If you dare, take a paper and pen, and in the quiet places begin to write from your stream of consciousness. Do not critique yourself; all is fair game. Explore the song within you.

SECTION 2: Creating and Birthing

4

Breasts

Taught from infancy that beauty is woman's scepter,
the mind shapes itself to the body, and roaming round its gilt cage,
only seeks to adorn its prison.

—MARY WOLLSTONECRAFT

Bras & Breastplates

MY MOTHER-IN-LAW HAS TURNED her head and covered her eyes with one
hand as she holds onto my six-month-old son. I laugh out loud that she
thinks I need privacy while the store clerk measures my bust for the correct bra size. My sister-in-law is also there in the dressing room, and she is
almost more eager than I am to know the correct size bra I should be wearing. The clerk explains to us that the seam of the bra should not be directly
under your armpit but run closer to the back of your arm, to provide proper
circulation. We three women at the ages of seventy, forty-two, and thirty-
eight years old, had never been measured for the correct bra size to wear.
We giggled like school girls through the mall after that lesson, talking about
our experiences with bra knowledge.

Bra shopping was not a rite of passage in my family. We did not go
shopping for a training bra, rather I used my older sister's hand me down
bras. As a teenager, breastplates, as armor, was the closest understanding I

had imagined for the purpose of a bra. All I really knew about breastplates were that they were used to protect soldiers when going to battle. If we explore the concept of breastplates, it is actually a pretty exhilarating way to think about bras. By definition, breastplates are "devices worn over the torso to protect it from injury, as an item of religious significance, or as an item of status."[1] The definition itself sounds so beautiful compared to the definition I had been told by my brother for a bra, "over the shoulder boulder holder." If I put on my bra every day as an item of clothing symbolizing protection or status, and even as an article of armor with religious significance, how might I have come to experience my breasts on my body? Come to find out, the breastplate was worn by the high priestess as a symbol of judgment. Biblically, El Shaddai speaks about God's breast as mountains and with the undertones of protection.[2] [3] The amount of spiritual concepts we could teach women about what it means to put on a bra is endless.

If bra to breastplate isn't enough for you, how have you come to be with the size of your breasts? As a young girl growing up, I never talked about my breasts with anyone. I didn't know what a "normal" size was supposed to be; I was unaware of what size breasts guys liked. My friend Amanda told me once, "As long as it's a handful, it is enough." Other than that, I was clueless to the purpose or expectations of my breasts. If anything, breasts were a nuisance to me. Playing sports my whole life, there was nothing more frustrating than having to scrape a sweaty, tight sports bra off after a game. If you had asked me when I was a teenager, I would have told you God's intention in creating breasts was to annoy women and make men stumble.

In her book *Honoring the Body*, Stephanie Paulsell writes: "Young people who have grown up learning that the body mirrors back to us something important about God and that the body's desires are a precious gift from God worth being sheltered and allowed to develop in freedom have a compass to help them negotiate the road to sexual maturity."[4] When women truly realize their breasts and their vaginas were created in the image of God, to display the mysteries and perfections of God, it gives permission to allow these body parts to develop in freedom and to be cared for well. Research tells us that when we honor our bodies and the stories our body parts hold, we develop a healthier psyche and sexuality. Women's

1. *Merriam-Webster Dictionary*, "Breastplate."
2. Biale, "The god with breasts."
3. Lewis, "Breastplate of the High Priest."
4. Paulsell, *Honoring the Body*, 140.

breasts often live within the dance of invisibility and visibility. We hide the breasts of our youth in hopes of not being objectified, though we will one day grow old and become incensed by our withered, sagging breasts that our culture does not long to look at. *Our sexual body parts are at war with being seen; we don't know if we should hate, hide, or enshrine the beauty they offer.* Breasts are a divine mystery. They offer comfort, nourishment, rest, and pleasure. Objectification is war against the purpose of our breasts. As women, we often wear our breasts like hidden shields of shame rather than breastplates of righteousness.

Satisfying Breasts

As a female growing up in the church, I did not find much teaching illuminating the beauty of my specific reproductive body parts. The female anatomy has multiple body parts that produce the essence life. Breasts are among these life-producing parts, commonly translated in the Bible as drinking from or giving drink. We often associate the breast as giving drink by lactation, literally giving milk to infants, but breasts are also referenced sexually as giving satiating drink. Proverbs 5:19 speaks about "letting her breasts satisfy at all times." Within sexuality, the breasts refresh and fully satisfy the husband. The breasts are referred to as a gift for them both to delight in. The word *dadeyah*, "her breasts," only occurs here and is equivalent to *dodeyah*, "her love"; and *satisfy* reads as "water thee," literally meaning *y'ravvuka*, "to drink largely," "to be satisfied with drink." In a culture where women's breasts are usually objectified, it is refreshing to see God had a deeper intent when designing breasts.

We must begin by clarifying that God is not a sexual being, neither man nor woman. Rather the Trinity is a spirit. In turn, sexuality is not a human projection, it is an expression of God's image by creating us with male and female body parts. We are made in God's image, not God in ours. God is pure spirit in which there is no place for the difference between the sexes. But the respective "perfections" of man and woman reflect something of the divine, infinite perfection of God. Thus, we must ask ourselves, what perfection of God is being portrayed by the woman's breast? Breasts sustain life.

Breast Pump

River, at three days old, is laying in the isolette with what looks to be Ray-Bans strapped to his face. The image would be the perfect advertisement for a tanning bed company, but unfortunately, it is because I birthed him five weeks early and we are spending the next thirty days boarded here in the hospital NICU. After the emergency C-section, he was taken immediately to the neonatal ICU. Although I was relieved at his safety, I sadly wasn't able to spend the first few hours with my baby. The doctors told me that when I could move my legs and walk to the NICU, I would be able to see him. I was desperate to wear off the anesthesia residing in my lower limbs, so I spent those hours distracting myself by squeezing colostrum into tiny syringes and sending them via my husband to give to my precious newborn. This was the beginning of a long season: being boarded in the hospital for a month, pumping every two hours, washing the equipment, measuring and fortifying the amounts exactly, and gavage feeding the breast milk into his premature belly. There were charts, calendars, and storage bags that were being constantly updated. Name, date, amount. Every two hours, again and again, name, date, amount.

The hours accrued in the rocking chair near his isolette seemed countless. Around the clock I would watch and wait for a moment to hold my four-pound little baby. When I would get him, I wouldn't let him go. It would be three hours at a time of skin to skin, before the nurses would beckon me to go back to pump or sleep. My body was so desperate to be near my baby; my heart was hungry to have him on my chest. I stared at all the machines monitoring his vitals. My body had done the work that the many machines filling an entire room were now doing. I have never been more in awe of the female body than at that moment of realization. The womb was as powerful as these medical machines, and my breast provided milk that was the perfect life source he needed for growth.

Momma's Milk

At three years of age, my oldest son Wilder is lying in his bed drinking a bottle, trying to fall asleep. I am lying with him while I nurse his baby sister during our bedtime routine. He watches me in deep thought. "Mom, how much momma milk can you make?" He is looking at me with sheer curiosity as I begin to calculate the usual ounces I can pump in one sitting. "Well buddy, I think I probably can make ten to twelve fluid ounces, which is a full bottle." His immediate impatience surprises me: "No, Mom, how much momma milk is inside of you?" I realize he is asking about *all* the milk my body is able to produce. I begin to calculate the last two years of feeding every few hours. He is frustrated with my math skills, and I stop calculating around 2,000 ounces. I know he wouldn't understand 2,000 so I say, "I have about 200 gallons of momma milk in me, my love." He is satisfied that I have given him an answer and is silent for a while. He finishes his own bottle and very quietly says, "Your body is amazing." While his reflection is so kind, it is his initial inquiry that was so intriguing to me, it awakened my own wonder. Also, my friend who is a lactation consultant had calculated her entire milk production through child-rearing years, so I calculated how much momma milk I produced for all three of my kids. Let's just say my body has been the barista of about 5,475 venti cups in my lifetime. That is the amount my body has produced over the past decade to nourish my three babies, I am in awe and exhausted by this thought. I have to agree with my son, breasts really are amazing.

Mastectomy

The rhythmic jerk of our little speedboat steadily rocked us back and forth as we crossed the Mekong River on a four-hour boat trek into the remote northern tip of Thailand. Aunt Jinx and I were taking an excursion to the Golden Triangle, the point where Laos, Thailand, and Myanmar meet. We had just finished teaching in the Chang Rai province. It had been my eight-year dream to finally meet the girl I sponsored through Compassion International, and my aunt took me on a graduation trip to meet my sponsored child. After meeting her, we spent the next two weeks traveling to learn about different native tribes of women in the area.

The first tribe we met were the White Karen tribe of women in Northern Chang Rai. Each woman was wearing multiple gold rings holding up her elongated neck and adorning her wrists. The number of golden rings is connected culturally to the status and beauty of the woman. I am intrigued by the commitment and capacity of these tribal women to live in these rural countries while raising children, yet still making space in their lives for markers of cultural beauty, such as colorful beaded work, metals made into jewelry, and vibrant dyed cloth. I find I am surprised at beauty being a sought-after commodity, even to women in the most rural locations.

My Aunt Jinx, on the other hand, is not a woman consumed with or seeking after physical beauty. Now, let me tell you about Aunt Jinx—she is quite a character. This is a woman with more life in her eyes than a kid in a candy store. Every day is magical to her, and every moment is an opportunity for goodness to be created. Aunt Jinx has no regard for filters and has been known to lift up her shirt and show her mastectomy scar at any family event. She survived breast cancer, and although we love hearing the story, we struggle to politely navigate her placing your hand on her breast-less chest, mid-conversation in her unabashed pride. We pretend not to notice her one exposed breast that peaks out when her breast scar is being displayed. To her credit, she makes sure that her missing breast won't be glossed over or ignored. Her survival scars speak of grit and bravery, and she will not allow them to be silenced. I admire that trait deeply.

Aunt Jinx was celebrating her eleventh year of remission from breast cancer, and, on this Asian trip, we learned that she had had a reoccurrence. This was a very sobering part of our trip as she wrestled again with the acceptance of potential death, but she continued traveling with determination to live life to the fullest. On this particular day, we were meeting a remote all female tribe on an island. As we docked the boat on a grass shore, the Hmong tribe stood there to greet us. We spent the afternoon with them and while few words were exchanged exploring this isolated and breathtaking island, we felt connected to these women and their land. As we prepared to leave, an older woman from the tribe hugged Aunt Jinx and noticed her missing breast. She patted her own chest where she, too, was missing a breast. They both put their hands on the other's scars and were silent for a moment. As a witness, I felt the weight of this moment, as these two unlikely strangers stopped and honored their connection through their scars. The woman pulled out a small emerald carved elephant with a raised trunk, which I came to find out symbolizes long life, and wrapped it within Aunt Jinx's hand. No words were spoken, yet volumes were communicated as both women shared this meaningful moment. Scars are a reminder that death did not take away one's life.

More Mastectomies

Lord, have mercy. I mouth the silent prayer as I listen to her muffled whimpers through the heavy metal restroom door. She has locked herself in the women's bathroom, which is located right outside my counseling office on the second floor of the oncology unit. Her double mastectomy surgery a week prior was successful—successful in the sense that the cancer was removed, along with her breast. She has had her first follow-up appointment and the bandages will be removed today, and then an aftercare plan made. The somber air is thick as another woman bears the image of her newly scarred and marked body. Where her breasts once were, she sees an imperfect diagonal suture line across her chest. She will no longer see the breast that she bought bras to fit, tugged blouses to cover, her bosom where lovers had nuzzled, her babies suckled. She stares, taking in the unjust barter of her beautiful breast replaced by a purplish-red scar. I wait patiently for her to reach composure and come join me for our therapy session. At this point, I have been an oncologist therapist for a little under a year and worked with a handful of women who had undergone mastectomies and double mastectomies. I journey with these women as they navigate the long road of processing what it means to have an appendage removed for the sake of continuing to live.

It is an emotionally disturbing process to be put to sleep and wake up without your breast, or any part of your body, for that matter. The sounds echoing from the recovery room bathroom are, at times, horrifying. Some women lock themselves in stalls and weep. Some women refuse to come out of surgery without having breast reconstruction the same day. Whatever a woman's reaction to the loss of her breast, it is difficult to navigate society's expectation, the healthy grieving process, and what it means to heal from the loss of our good body. Much research shows mastectomy as a lifesaving treatment for many women, yet there is little research on the post-mastectomy symptoms. As with other surgeries, there is often painful scarring as a result of the trauma on the body. In addition, there is a negative impact to the patient's sexuality and body image.[5] The loss of a body part takes time to process, grieve, and become accustomed to. There is an emotional component tied to the loss of a body part, as intimate as our connective tissue visibly showing the severance of an appendage. In the medical field, the stress response is the hormonal and metabolic changes in the body following injury or trauma, such as surgery. Research confirms that our bodies hold trauma in our sinew and tissue, and we are able to see the trauma much like scar tissue around a once-severed site. The body remembers what anesthesia numbs or erases, and often our minds block out. In his book *The Body Keeps the Score*, Dr. Bessel van der Kolk explains, "Long

5. Davies et al., "Exploring the Lived Experience."

after a traumatic experience is over, it may be reactivated at the slightest hint of danger and mobilize disturbed brain circuits and secrete massive amounts of stress hormones."[6]

It does not have to be the extreme of a mastectomy or constructive surgery; our breasts hold stories. With every female client who comes into my office, at some point during therapy I pose the questions: "What is the story of your breasts? What would your breasts, or any reproductive part of your body, tell me if they could speak? What has it been like living as a part of your body?"

These questions are not limited to your breasts. They apply to any reproductive part of your body, such as womb, vagina, or pelvic floor. As women, God has built our bodies with magnificent reproductive abilities: our breasts lactate, our clitoris orgasms, our uterus creates life. All of these incredible parts of our bodies are invitations to know and understand our Creator. God was so kind when he invited women to co-create life with him. This invitation, this gift of our reproducing body parts, is also very vulnerable and susceptible. We, as women, are invited to know the story of our body parts—in particular, the reproductive ones—in order to understand God in a deeper way. Having worked in the psychological world of women for over ten years now, I am keenly aware of how many times evil moves to strike the woman's reproductive body parts as a way to minimize or silence them. Women must study the wounds, scars, and triumphs of our bodies inside and out, thus meeting a God who created us perfectly in her image.

Bravely bearing the wounds and scars of our body takes the deepest work of the soul. Our body was given to invite us into the act of creation. The human body is capable of creating the joys of art, pleasure, and health. Conversely, we must understand that the body's greatest battle is to bear grief well when it is wounded or severed. How we address the scars of our bodies is crucial to our emotional health. It is important to identify the scars on our bodies, physical and emotional, and to know their origin in detail. Scar stories give us insight into the themes of our woundedness and recovery. If we are mindful, they give us information on what our bodies are capable of enduring and, ultimately, what our bodies can know and experience.

My time working in the oncology unit was harrowing, as burned and mutilated bodies are enormously costly to bear, work with, and aid in

6. Van Der Kolk, *The Body Keeps the Score,* 14.

healing. There is one patient whose story has stayed with me these past ten years. After a double mastectomy, this woman returned to my counseling office with her husband, desperately trying to save her marriage of thirty-two years. As she and her husband sat in my office, they told me that sex did not seem possible anymore. Her husband reported that every time he saw the scars across her chest, he wanted to vomit. I restrained myself from shuddering when he stated flatly, "I definitely can't get it up to have sex when I see those scars." These were my early years as a therapist, and while I hid my disgust at his honesty and callousness, I was at a loss. Immediately after the session, I consulted with my supervisor. I needed direction to work effectively with this couple. I couldn't think of how to help this couple see hope in this situation. My wise supervisor was clear and confident in her response. She explained that *scars become our body's most intimate invitations*. Deeper than genitalia, the marks on our body where we barely escaped death are the most powerful conduits for intimacy. I will never forget Tina's supervision about this subject. She said, "To allow someone to enter our wounds is to allow someone to enter the most intimate place, more intimate than any orgasm." Her words were profound, and I believed her. I went back with confidence to continue working with my distressed couple.

Scar Stories

All scar stories of trauma and hardship have power. Intimacy is in the sharing of painful places. Engaging our own intimacy within our own bodies and scars are the first steps. Writing down the stories of your reproductive body parts and how they have been scarred is a great place to start on your road to knowing God through your body's story. When I stand bare before a mirror, I know the curves, scars, stretch marks that my body has endured. I know what I think about those places, and I have asked God to name what those stories have meant to him. Naming these places allows us to make meaning of how our calling is being informed from our life events. God is aware of the details: *he knows every hair on our head,*[7] *he holds every one of our tears in a jar,*[8] and *he knit us in our mother's womb;*[9] God intimately knows the details of our bodies and our scars. From this place, I am able to

7. Luke 12:7.
8. Psalm 56:8.
9. Psalm 139:13–14.

choose to offer my husband the invitation of knowing what my body has endured and how he can know me more intimately. When a committed and safe spouse is able to know the stories of your body's scars, there is an invitation to deeper intimacy. The sharing and co-bearing of our agony is the fearful and sacred road to true connection and intimacy. This tension is a beautiful journey when we engage what has been asked of our bodies.

Chapter 4 Questions: Breasts

1. What do you believe is God's reason for creating your breasts?

2. If you asked your breasts to tell the story of what it is like to be on your body, what would the story be?

3. What are you scar stories, and can you see themes in what your body has survived or continued to hold inside that needs to be released? Scan your body and note all the places where there are scars; be curious of what these stories are.

Scar Intimacy Exercise:

All scar stories of trauma and hardship have power. Intimacy is in the sharing of places of pain. Engaging our own intimacy within our own bodies and scars are the first steps. How do you engage your own scarred body and how do you invite a partner into that space? Have you ever touched the scars on your body with intention? Have you ever allowed your partner to touch the scars on your body? Writing down the stories of your reproductive body parts and how they have been marred or scarred is a great place to start on your road to knowing God through your body's story.

5

A Sexual God

Insofar as the body is a site of divine presence
(seen most definitely in the Incarnation),
women must see their wombs and erotic energy as a sacrament.
We must teach young women and girls to feel
the pleasure, pain, sadness, and creativity
that is bubbling up from their pelvic bowl and their sexual organs
and greet these sensations as teachers,
not as shameful enemies.

—KAREN ROSS, *Womb Energy and Erotic Justice for Women and Girls*

Delight of the Body

HER DRAMATICALLY CUT, DARK hair is moving back and forth just past her chin as she shakes her head no. I have been working in my counseling practice with this client for over a year now, targeting her lack of emotion when it comes to her desire. Our therapy sessions are proactive and logistical, her gut response rigid to join the conversations. She has grown to trust me, sharing stories of deep betrayal and hurt, yet her face is set, her frame always composed as if she doesn't feel the pain she articulates. It dawns on me that her stories of shame and legalism are often stories of her and her mother. I ask her, why is it that she can discipline self-care for her physical body, but she cannot engage her emotional sadness or sensual desires? Immediately, a story of shame and nakedness she told early in our work comes back to me. I hear her repeating her mother's words out loud when catching her daughter innocently delighting in her body, "Ladies don't act that way." Take note, evil is subtle and simple when it can be; so, you are likely to overlook it. Over and over, I have come to recognize that evil is spoken over us and we agree and make a vow. Evil is not complex if it doesn't need to be because it doesn't want to be exposed. Evil is dark, subtle, and mean. This client still believes her mother's words; she is still mothering herself just as she was taught, with a sterile and conforming distance to her own body. We began to unwrap the shame and embarrassment around her body's pleasure and vulnerability. We realized that she had no idea how to mother herself into being a woman. She had never been allowed to explore and delight in her body without shame. She had never been taught to be imaginative and listen, to mark and honor her body. We have defined shame as a belief that there is something wrong with us, and so to not feel that shame we will turn to self-contempt or other-centered contempt. Contempt is an effective way to make delight and glory pay for showing up in our body. We can hate ourselves or the other's body, we make it evil and therefore, we cannot love or delight in our own pleasure and glory. In these moments, we join evil and obliterate ourselves or others because it is easier than joining God, who fearfully and wonderfully made us.

Historical Sexuality and God's Design

Doctors, therapists, parents, teachers, and pastors have trouble openly talking and teaching about sex. Sex is a powerful and difficult subject to explore through the eyes of God. Most churches have little education on who is equipped to navigate the conversations of sexuality and God, other than mandating abstinence. God's design for sex is obviously intentional and powerful, and I believe God has given us power through the holiness involved in the act of sex and pleasure. My professor and mentor for many years, Dr. Tina Schermer Sellers, is a Christian Certified Sex Therapist who trains Christian therapists on how to counsel clients around healthy sexuality. She teaches about the history and practices of the Law of Onah,[1] laws directed mainly to men, which command the man to give his wife pleasure

---

1. Sellers, "Vow of Onah."

during sexual acts, not to just think of himself. Research records these laws from the Torah, specifically outlining a sexual principle that protects women as a direct rule:

> Sexual relations should only be experienced in a time of joy. Sex for selfish personal satisfaction, without regard for the partner's pleasure, is wrong and evil. A man may never force his wife to have sex. A couple may not have sexual relations while drunk or quarreling. Sex may never be used as a weapon against a spouse, either by depriving the spouse of sex or by compelling it. It is a serious offense to use sex (or lack thereof) to punish or manipulate a spouse. Sex is the woman's right, not the man's. Although sex is the woman's right, she does not have absolute discretion to withhold it from her husband.[2]

These laws invite us to begin the exploration of God's design for sex as it relates to pleasure and spirituality. It was during my first seminary class discussion that my professor mentioned that the female clitoris is the size of a pencil eraser but has more nerve endings than the head of the male penis. I was shocked; no one had ever told me that. She posed the question, "Why would God give women a clitoris which only has the physiological function to receive pleasure?" I researched the function of the clitoris, finding it described as an extremely sensitive organ made up of erectile tissue that has thousands of nerve endings, with its central function being to produce sensations of sexual pleasure. I was stunned to confirm that the clitoris, in fact, has no function in reproduction and has 8,000 nerve endings, which is double to amount of the nerve endings on the penis. *Who knew seminary could be so helpful?* This information has been a stunning revelation for thousands of students and clients that I work with. We are under-educated as a Christian population about God's design of the female body, especially concerning sexuality. How can we expect to build a healthy theology around God's plan for sexuality if we don't study his design of our sexual organs?

While the female body requires obvious honor and awe, objectification of the female body at the woman's expense brings death. If a woman's reproductive, life-creating body parts, which are created in God's image, are objectified, it prevents her body from being engaged with the way God intended. Rob Bell describes Christian sexuality as a dance between being "angel," a spirit without a body, or "animal," a body that lives by basic

2. Mamre, "Torah 101," 2.

instinct. Bell writes about how we, as believers, must live as humans, neither angel or animal, but somewhere in between:

> Angels were here before us. Animals were here before us. When we act like angels or animals, we're acting like beings who were created before us. We're going backwards in creation. We're going the wrong way . . . Our actions, then, aren't isolated. Nothing involving sex exists independent of and disconnected from everything around it. How we act determines the kind of world we're creating. And with every action, we're continuing the ongoing creation of the world. The question is, what kind of world are we creating? How we live matters because God made us human. Which means we aren't angels. And we aren't animals.[3]

The question he asks is applicable to every person, at every juncture of life: *what kind of world are we creating?* In the context of our sexuality, we must ask ourselves this question. Do we see sexuality as something to fear, or have we trusted that God intended sexuality as a powerful tool for creating? How do we use our sexuality for the glory of God? How do we use our bodies for creating? The secular culture leads us to believe that we are animals (i.e., over-sexualized) and often the church leads us to believe we are angels (i.e., asexual). In particular, the woman's body through pregnancy demands that we see that sex is designed to create life. What kind of a world are you creating, one of objectification or true intimacy?

Objectification: Gray Matter

My husband has a brilliant red T-shirt that reads, "porn kills love." I will tell you that, if anything, it is a conversation starter whenever he wears it. My husband also is a therapist who specializes in porn addiction. I am a therapist who specializes in healthy sexuality, so you can see we are constantly around conversations and research about sexual harm and sexual health. It wasn't surprising to me when I woke up one night after a jarring sexual dream. In the dream, I was watching a man masturbate as he looked at pornography on a computer screen. There was gray ash-like matter coming from his moving hand and drifting into the air, much like fog from pollution. In the next moment, I was suspended into the night atmosphere as I watched the gray matter slough off of houses all through the city. The gray matter filled the atmosphere like smog in a major industrial city. In the

3. Bell, *Sex God*, 63–64.

dream, I become aware that women all over the world are breathing in this toxic haze, and it is making them deathly sick. It turns into a nightmare, and I begin to feel like I am suffocating from the claustrophobic pollution, waiting for a call from my husband to tell me where to go to find safety from the polluted air. There are men looking for me, and I know they are trying to find and rape me. My husband finally calls, and through the broken-up reception he explains that the gray matter is killing women everywhere. It fills their lungs and their bodies, and they are dying. I hear the men who are chasing me getting closer and I start running. The dream ends when my husband tells me that he will never see me again but that I must run to the forest's edge where my sister is waiting to drive us across the border. I run, but before I can make it to her, I am captured by the men and raped to my death. I wake up screaming.

Whew. Take a deep breath. It is a sobering and intense dream.

Because I work with women who are partnered with sex addicts, much of the transference my brain attempts to regulate comes from years of working with stories about sexual trauma and abuse. Thankfully, I have had some training in dream analysis, and as a therapist who often works with the realms of sexuality, I know a bit about how to navigate this dream. I woke up and wrote for hours after I had this particular dream. Evil felt very near. The dream's narrative speaks to why I believe we as Christians absolutely must understand sexuality. God created sexuality with power in mind, power for good. Evil has had other ideas of how to use sexuality for harm, hate, and darkness. Sexual assault, rape, and incest are prevalent in our world. One out of every three women have been sexually abused. *Evil would not be running rampant with sexual harm if sexuality weren't just as powerful a weapon for good.* Again, evil would not have the ability do so much harm with sexuality if God had not created it with the intent of empowerment. Would God have created sex if he had known how much pain and harm it would bring? Our Creator had a plan, a good one, when he designed sex.

For weeks after, I pondered my dream and what could combat this "gray matter" from sexual harm, if indeed it were poisoning us. I spent a few weeks reading peer-reviewed research on the effects of pornography on women's sexuality and health. There is cause to believe the effects of an objectifying society can be seen in the deterioration of women and their health. How could we stop this? What counteracts this destructive gray matter? My answer is holy intimacy and sex, or what I call gold dust.

Intimacy: Gold Dust

There is a small corner in North Seattle, the intersection of 90th and Aurora Avenue to be exact, where my church runs a neighborhood ministry for sexually trafficked women. These are women who spend their lives selling sex for money, food, and drugs. You can imagine the sexual harm and trauma these women have endured and witnessed. I spend time with them every first Wednesday of the month, and they teach me about God in more ways than I ever imagined. They teach me about hope and resilience, but even more they teach me about what combats this gray matter of sexual harm. *Gold dust* is the term I have given to what I believe is produced when someone engages in sexual health. Sexuality is objectified in society and shamed and/or silenced in the Christian world. As believers, we must learn the power of holy and healthy sexuality. Pope John Paul II wrote an entire book on the subject, *The Theology of the Body: Human Love in the Divine Plan*, in which he states:

> Man thus ceases to live as a person and a subject. Regardless of all intentions and declarations to the contrary, *he becomes merely an object*. This neo-Manichaean culture has led, for example, to human sexuality being regarded more *as an area for manipulation and exploitation* than as the basis of that primordial *wonder* which led Adam on the morning of creation to exclaim before Eve: "This at last is bone of my bones and flesh of my flesh" (Gen. 2:23). This same wonder is echoed in the words of the Song of Solomon: "You have ravished my heart, my sister, my bride, you have ravished my heart with a glance of your eyes."[4]

We must realize that we are not objects for manipulation and exploitation; the body is something of wonder. Good sex, life-giving sex, metaphorically emits a gold dust into the atmosphere. Of course, there is no scientific research affirming the existence of gray matter or gold dust, but the imagery is helpful when considering the effects of sexuality in the realm of spiritual warfare. Let us return to my seminary professor's question: what is God's design for sexuality? It can't only be reproduction, otherwise he would never have given women a clitoris. Remember, the clitoris has no

4. Pope John Paul II, *Man and Woman*, 3.

other biological function than to give pleasure. God was intentional when he created the clitoris, a body part that is only for pleasure and this pleasure has to have a spiritual component, which I believe is spiritual power. As I pondered these concepts, I eventually began to envision that gold dust could dissipate the gray matter. It took me twelve years of research to answer my professor's question. I believe God created the clitoris for sexuality to play a role in defeating evil.

Gold dust is life. Gray matter is death.

Encounter and Bless

True intimacy invites us into the divine. Technology is a false example of intimacy, and pornography is a false example of sexuality. We have come to replace our real human experiences with counterfeits that are keeping us from the true design God intended our bodies to experience. In his book *Anam Cara*, John O'Donohue writes,

> The Bible says that no one can see God and live. In a transferred sense, no person can see himself and live. All you can ever achieve is a sense of your soul. You gain little glimpses of its light, color, and contours. You feel the inspiration of its possibilities and the wonder of its mysteries. In the Celtic tradition, and especially in the Gaelic language, there is a refined sense of the sacredness that the approach to another person should embody. The word hello does not exist in Gaelic. The way that you encounter someone is through blessing. You say, *Dia Dhuit,* God be with you. The response, *Dia is Muire dhuit,* God and Mary be with you. When you are leaving a person, you say, *Go gcumhdai Dia thu,* May God come to your assistance or *Go gcoinne Dia thu,* May God keep you. The ritual of encounter is framed at the beginning and at the end with blessing.[5]

The word hello does not exist in Gaelic.

The way you encounter someone is through giving and receiving blessing.

5. O'Donohue, *Anam Cara*, 16–18.

I find myself simultaneously intrigued and turned off by this statement. No one says "hello," rather, gives a blessing? Wow. Will we as a society
learn to bless ourselves and each other instead of making the human soul
an object? Consider the work it takes to make eye contact and say a blessing
when you see someone. The exhausted woman in me cringes at the thought
of using my imagination and energy to bless someone, rather than sit on
my phone and click "like" on forty of my friends' social media accounts.

In my house, we have been working on saying "excuse me" when walking through crowds while in public places. My three-year-old looks directly
in strangers' eyes and yells "Excuse me!" with pride and confidence. My
six-year-old, on the other hand, looks down and mumbles the words as we
move through the masses. I sometimes come down to his level and ask him
to speak up and make eye contact with the person we are walking past. He
exposes the wrestling it takes in the work of encountering the other.

To bless someone is intimate; it produces intimacy between the two
blessing each other.

To encounter is to take someone in and be invited to the sensuality
and often sexuality of the other person. Inviting someone in gives them ac-
cess to the reality of who you are, displacing the fantasy. Connection leads
to the vulnerability of being accepted or rejected. In long term relationships, continued vulnerability can be difficult as domestication of monogamous relationships seems less enticing. In a research study on the levels of
oxytocin in rats' brains, studies showed that oxytocin never spiked higher
than at the initial time a rat mated with another rat. Monogamy offered
little opportunity for heightened arousal, but when a new rat partner was
introduced, oxytocin once again spiked. For parturient and lactating rats,
oxytocin was elevated after birth and during breastfeeding. The conclusion
of the study showed a defeating result for monogamous couples: your oxytocin likely doesn't ever spike higher than the first time you kiss or have sex,
except during breastfeeding, and acts of near death experiences. Thus, the
term "mating in captivity" brings a difficult challenge to keeping the love
alive in your marriage, particularly on a hormonal level. I tell many of my
clients in relationship that they are brave to be their partner's reality and
not their fantasy.

If there is room for me to push you further into this idea, I might
venture to say in particular to women's sexuality, God created it with a purpose. Our voice and our sexual pleasure are part of our calling to live a holy
life. There is something in the beauty of a woman's body that reminds all

humans of glory. This glory is most personified when it resonates deeply with our own beauty and a clear remembering of where we come from. The power of the female gender is living and wild. We have the power to save the world through God-ordained pleasure, healthy sexuality, and the belief that love defeats all evil and death. *There is no war, no death, no hopelessness that can take away what the power of love can do.* I believe women hold this truth deep inside of them.

Blessing the Sexually Wounded Place

It has been three weeks since the D&C. There is little bleeding, if any, and I am crying in my husband's arms. The kids are asleep, and we are attempting to have sex, but I can't stop crying. Sex is such an act of the present. My body and mind are timid and scared. My vagina remembers what my mind can't articulate: three weeks ago the pieces of our lifeless child were taken through this passageway and now my husband wants to enter this same place. Truly, this is not a moment I can explain completely, yet my choices are to either engage and share this deep sadness with myself and my partner, or to silence this great grief and not offer him any invitation to intimacy. Sex is still such a taboo conversation in the church, yet there is such a power and holiness in sex that is not taught. When we offer our stretched skin and scarred bodies, we are offering the greatest invitation to intimacy. When we bring our history of wounded heartaches and our broken pieces to another person again and again, we are invited into the holy of holies. What has come to be mating in captivity can be an invitation to the most intimate place.

The holy of holies is the inner chamber of a sanctuary, separated by a thin veil—a place believed to be the most sacred and to be entered to receive atonement. I cannot prove that God made a woman's vagina to represent this place, but there is something so sacred to be invited to enter into a person's body. I remember going into the hospital to birth my second child and my OBGYN wanted to try to break my water. She looked at me straight in the eyes, her lavender gloved hand ready, and she said, "Christy, I am going into God's country now." I laughed out loud. Yet her words ring clear in my mind. There was a jovial honoring that she was going to enter my body with reverence to check on the baby ready to be birthed. Her recognition, as a doctor, was that something divine had created my uterus and my vagina and it was a holy place. Our vaginas are not to be entered or engaged without honor and awe; it is an invitation to the holy of holies.

Sadly, I have the honor of working with many women who have had some type of sexual harm done to their bodies. Whether by childhood sexual abuse, domestic violence, rape, or trauma, I sit with hundreds of women who have received scars in the most sacred place inside of their bodies. Sometimes these memories don't surface until decades later when they are engaged in some type of physical act: sex, birth, a painful period, etc. Once these stories emerge we begin the process of psychological surgery in which we clean out a wound and re-suture. Our bodies want to heal and if we follow a few practices, our bodies will recover. This process can only be done when we honor our wounding by grieving and burying what has died. My husband and I were ambivalent around intimacy and pleasure during our grief about our stillborn son; we had no guide on how to offer our traumatized bodies to each other in the holy and pleasurable act of sex. We had to first grieve together before we were able to find any pleasure in this sacred place. Sex needed to become something more than pleasure and an act of procreation. *Sex had to become the most powerful prayer where both grief and pleasure could co-exist.*

During a podcast interview with my friend and author Beth Bruno, she made a statement about the parallel between the way of suffering Christ walked within the woman's body. She said, "I just pictured as you spoke about the theology of the womb, that the vaginal canal is like the Via Dolorosa, the way of suffering. It is the place in the woman's body that is the path from death into life." I was taken aback by her imagery, because yes, she was naming so clearly what I have come to find true, the place in which death and life pass within a woman's body is her vaginal canal. Blessing the wounded sexual place requires one's partner to enter her most wounded area, the vaginal canal. This imagery of entering each others' wounded places, through sex, is mimicked with Christ's invitation to understanding the *cost and gift* of co-creating. It is a part of the sacrament of marriage. Sex and marriage invite us to know co-creation with our Creator. Individually, as women, we are being offered an invitation to know God as Creator through the cycle of our womb.

Chapter 5 Questions: Sexuality

1. What do you believe God's purpose was when he created your sexual organs and sexual pleasure?

2. What do you think about your clitoris only being created to give you pleasure, as it has no other physiological function?

3. What is your understanding of God's hope and plan for sexuality in this world as a Christian?

4. How do you engage your sexual health, sexual pleasure, and the power of God's design for your sexuality?

6

God as Womb

Since the moment the little humans leave my body,
parenthood feels like a series of goodbyes.

—MEL PARSONS

Pray to Let Go

LIVING IN THE PACIFIC Northwest, but coming from the Deep South, a Christian attains a spectrum of friends who come from very different theologies. It is quite the journey in relationships holding both types of faith equally in your friendships. I have friends who would never believe in or go to a church with a female pastor, while I have friends who are female pastors. I have friends who prophesy over me in other tongues and those who will have a Catholic mass said on my behalf. Truly, I learn so much from each of these friendships, all offering me different aspects of the *imago Dei*. There is one friend in particular, Nicole, who has the best Southern accent and is the mother of four girls. She is the spunkiest, most charismatic Christian friend I have. This woman hears from the Lord and speaks with a boldness of 10,000 Spirit-filled prophetesses. She coached me through dating and marrying my husband and when we were ready for kids she told me clearly, "Christy, when you even start to think about wanting children, start praying for the strength to let go."

The strength to let go, how wise those words. Mothers are invited to know God in ways I can't begin to convince you of. After birthing your child's life from your body, there is no strength but God's strength that allows a momma to give her child back to the ultimate Creator. *Start praying for the strength to let go.* Can you hear God the Father praying for the strength to let go of his Son? What divine power did it take to let Jesus go into a human woman's womb and be birthed into a sinful world? All the while knowing that his young deity would be slaughtered to death and God the Father would have to turn his face. Turn his face away from his dying Son and not save him. Parents are asked to set their children free in a world that is not safe. Mothers are invited to know a little more of what God went through to create and birth a child and then let him go.

God's Hands

It has been at least three minutes since the doctor told me I could stop pushing. There is a spotlight at the end of the bed, but the room is otherwise dark. The epidural made it so that even in delivering him breach, I wasn't sure when he had fully come out of me. At this point, I have known for almost twenty-eight hours now that I would be delivering a baby that was not alive. Yet the delivery room is so very quiet, and the hushed voices are strained. My husband, whose face has been near mine, looks quietly defeated. I break the awkward silence with a chilling desperation in my voice that even I didn't recognize.

"Can I see him?" I bravely ask.

The room remains eerily still. My doctor's voice is steady and clear. "Alyssa is holding him until we can suture you a little more." The response is less than desirable and I feel the weight of the next passing minutes lay heavy on my empty chest. I trust Alyssa to hold him, she is my friend, she is my doula, of course she will hold him carefully and sweetly until I am allowed. Even though I know my son's heart stopped beating over thirty-six hours ago, the desire to rush him to a crash cart the moment I delivered him pounds in my mind. Yet no one is moving fast. On the contrary, everyone is moving painfully slow. I have been waiting to meet him for nine months now, to see his face and note whether it looks like mine or his father's. I will wait longer, while they unwind the umbilical cord one, two, three, four times from around his neck and again from around his chest. His life strangled in my womb. My son's life taken where it was given. Death in the most sacred and safe place.

Few women are ever handed their child not breathing.
Very few women birth death.

Death was not ever meant to come before the day of birth, never. When this happens, it is always wrong and always a horrible accident. The Creator of life is not about death; the Creator of life defeated death by resurrection. I am not as deep a woman of faith as these next few paragraphs will convey, but I am a woman of deep hope. When they handed me my sweet lifeless son, I kissed him, and prayed life would come back to his body. I rubbed his little hands and feet begging God to bring a heartbeat back. Twelve hours into the darkest of days, after friends and family had come to see him, hold him, baptize him, we gave him back to the nurse. My wrestling heart did not give up, even when we buried him in the graveyard, I told the Lord I believed he could still come back to life. Days turned into months and I would return mercilessly to the grave site and lay my hands on the cold, hard ground and believe life could be restored. *But in a world yet to be redeemed, all those who create must face death.*

Watching a mother bury her creation is a chilling act to observe. After a child dies, people don't know what to do. We had all kinds of reactions from our communities: meals upon meals, grocery bags upon grocery bags for days were left on our doorstep. Some people didn't come at all, some relatives didn't call, write, or respond. For the majority, people seemed to be waiting on us to tell them what to do, yet it was our world that had shattered. By the kindest of mercies, our community did not leave us; they demanded to be near. We spent the first week in our pastor's house, sleeping in their bed. They moved out and close friends of ours slept in all different rooms in their house, just to be near us. There was weeping ongoing for the first few days, tears met on each other's faces whether in the kitchen, living room, or bedrooms. We grieved continually with soft voices. A sign was hung on the door, "house of mourning." We wept, we had visitors, we had people rub our feet, shave my husband's hair, dread our son's hair into my own hair. We kept a fire continually burning. When it came time for the funeral, we took ash from the fireplace and put the sign of the cross on each other's foreheads. We tore clothing, we told stories, we sat in silence, we visited the grave . . . and then we did it all over again the next day.

We were posed a question a few weeks later from our spiritual mentor: "What is it you want to do with death?" My answer was fierce, immediate, and derived from a barren and courageous womb. *I want to mock death.* This is what I believe is being asked of every one of us. Truly, we have all birthed death at some level, and we are being asked what will we do about it? Will we create again? Will we create knowing that life is not the promised result? How will we live toward resurrection when it has yet to come for us here on earth? The gift of death is to know the importance and beauty of the presence with another. The gift of death is the reminder of eternal life, we remember through the act of communion.

Communion: Remembering to Create

"I WANT YOU BODY OF CHRIST!" I yelled. This is the phrase that echoed through the silent cathedral as my mom made her way back to the pew where she had been sitting before communion. I was only two years old at the time she carried me in her arms to receive communion at mass. The priest blessed my forehead with the sign of the cross and served my mother the Eucharist in her opened mouth, as her arms were full. As she walked back to her seat, my voice boomed aloud, "I WANT YOU BODY OF CHRIST!" I had jammed my hand into her mouth trying to retrieve the holy wafer. She was mortified, but we all laugh at the story now when she tells it. The story holds much meaning and mystery for me. I have always longed for and wanted to have the body of Christ in me. Communion has continued to digest in me over the cyclical phases of my life.

Early on in faith, there would never be a receiving of communion without tears running down my face. Many times, I didn't even understand why but I knew the tears signified my heart was contrite and ready to receive atonement. As time moved on, marriage brought on a different lens to sharing and breaking bread. Then, I lost my son Brave and communion felt like too much to bear, too much to receive. There were no tears, there was utter and overwhelming waiting and longsuffering hope that came every time a pastor or priest broke bread. For my body had been broken and poured out and death was laid into my arms. Easter was spent at a graveyard rather than a church building, for I couldn't leave my son's body to wonder why we all rejoiced when he was separated from us. Time follows if we keep breathing. After that season of death, I birthed two living children and I began to open my mouth again to receive the Eucharist, as now I had known more life than death after breaking flesh and being poured out.

Why did our Creator invite women have such an intimate part in creating life?

It is such a costly invitation. Jacques Ellul speaks about how the Creation story ends with God creating a woman. A woman who will later birth a Savior. Thus, women's birthright of old is one of co-creating a redemption story by birthing life. Somehow in this invitation, woman created from a rib at the end of the creation story finds herself continuing creation by building life within her womb.

Pregnancy Test: Vulnerability and Hope

My sister is waiting in the pharmacy register line as I hastily walk up to add to her pile of goods, with my hands full of Epsom salts and lavender oils. Before I put my products down she awkwardly turns and tells me to go to the other register to pay. If not for her quick change in demeanor, I wouldn't have looked down and noticed a box of pregnancy tests among her items to purchase. With indignation I try to hide my excitement and curiosity. I want to guard this time for her, I want to give her the adequate space needed.

Every woman remembers every time she has taken a positive pregnancy test. Let me tell you about pregnancy tests: they used to be weird. You were given a small, plastic stick to gather mid-stream urine. That is correct—I said mid-stream, you don't want the first urine or the last, you are instructed to catch mid-stream. We all know that accuracy is best with the first morning pee, but really, who is instructing us about mid-stream quality urine? Anyway, a woman collects her urine. Once that stick is coated in urine, the minute you wait to find your result is a very long sixty seconds. The liquid saturates the square and you watch for the latitudinal line to form. Thank God we have digital pregnancy tests now, which blink, blink, blink and as quickly as you wonder if the answer will come it blatantly stares back at you . . . PREGNANT or NOT PREGNANT. I do remember the feeling of waiting and then once the answer came, the spinning barrage of thoughts that filled the space. Will I ever get pregnant? Will I just keep trying or get medical help? I can't believe I am pregnant! Will it be a boy or girl? Will the baby be healthy? How do I tell my spouse? The race is on if there is a pregnancy sign, because as soon as it reads PREGNANT, you are immediately a parent.

My sister was actually pregnant in that story. She told me the next day, after she told her husband. It is a second child for them, so the questions, although a little less constant as with a first pregnancy, are different and still demanding. I feel myself pull away from the vulnerability tugging at my chest . . . it's not my baby, it isn't my pregnancy, it is my sister's. I know that a pregnancy makes us all vulnerable. If she loses their baby, they will be devastated. Truth is, after a family knows loss of a baby, any attempt after to create life is a possibility for devastation. Vulnerability is defined as when someone is capable of being physically or emotionally wounded. Creating life, attempting to create anything, makes us vulnerable. We become susceptible to losing it, destroying it, and God forbid, burying it. There is no way to create without vulnerability, there is no pregnancy test bought without vulnerability being purchased. Yes or no, relief or joy, life or blood . . . all pulse vulnerability through our veins.

In pregnancy, a woman is invited yet impotent in many ways to create life. We bear hormonal changes and reconfiguring of our body, yet we don't have to remember the week the heart needs to start beating, or how to grow limbs or organs; we just hold and contain. We have very little control over the life being created in us except for a few basic rules: no smoking and no drinking alcohol. Yet any week, any month of a pregnancy, we could go to the bathroom and find blood.

Death mocks our hope.
Death mocks our desire to create life.

God as Womb

In a spontaneous church service, a worship leader began repeating these words until she lead her entire church in prophetic worship to a song later titled *Surrounded*. Her words echoed in the large auditorium over and over,

It may look like I'm surrounded,
But I'm surrounded by You.
It may look like I'm surrounded,
But I'm surrounded by You.
This is how I fight my battles.[1]

1. Elyssa, "Surrounded."

This song later became a battle cry through my last pregnancy. Many hours I would sit in my therapy office listening to women struggle through the trauma and pain of miscarriage and pregnancy loss. At times, I would force myself to stop listening for a second, take a deep breath, and imagine a silver shield covering my entire body and protecting the small fetus growing within me. When anxiety or fear would creep in, I would play this song as loud as I could on repeat. The words felt representative of what the small child inside of me was experiencing, being surrounded by, yes, my uterus and nourished by my placenta, but even more surrounded by me, its life-source, its mother, its creator. In my fear and anxiety, I began to trust a theology of the womb, that I, this child's mother, had little control but was surrounded in the womb of God. God carries each of us in a womb, and women, in turn, have been invited into the understanding of carrying a child in our womb. I am surrounded by the great Creator, the most nurturing Mother. We as children of God are surrounded by something larger than ourselves. We do not enter this world alone or weak, our growing hearts are protected and surrounded by the all-knowing Creator of the universe. In the womb, we co-create with God, and we learn the hope in creating life and the loss of birthing death.

Infertility and Loss of Hope

Nineteen, twenty, twenty-one little yellow birds perched in a tree. Four are painted blue with life and the other seventeen painted yellow with loss. The framed picture in my sister-in-law's living room of twenty-one birds in a tree signify her family, seventeen yellow painted birds representing her children in heaven and four blue painted birds signifying her children on this earth. The verse in Ephesians is printed clearly underneath the tree, which reads, "to Him who is able to do *exceedingly abundantly* beyond all that we ask or think." She often remarks that abundance is different than she originally thought. Reproduction was a long road for Wendi, filled with years of giving herself injections, taking pills and medication for hormonal increase, countless waiting room and doctor visits. The agony of waiting and waiting to know if these embryos took, wondering if the implantations were successful. The warrior of a woman it takes to live through this process astounds me. The Proverb that often comes to mind when faced with a longing unfulfilled reads, "Hope deferred makes the heart sick, but a longing fulfilled is a tree of life."[2] How many sick hearts I have encountered over the years. I've endured my own sick heart at many seasons in my life, but the heart of a woman who longs for children and cannot have them has been one of the sickest hearts I have ever known. The women I have seen for therapy or done life with through seasons of infertility, miscarriage, or a child's death have been the heaviest of hearts.

The Waiting Womb

When we paused our work some eight months ago it was so she could focus on marriage counseling with her partner and try to get pregnant. I am aware when she walks into my office that she isn't pregnant. We begin the session and I ask her what it is she needs.

"I don't know, work is good. Work is great."

We both know she works with women who are having babies, so I immediately note that work cannot be good. I tell her it seems cruel to her to be working in her field and not be pregnant yet. Her head bows down in her hands, she begins sweeping tears away. "Why have I always wanted to have babies and I can't?"

In my work with clients, we often come upon a holy ground of warring with the trauma of one's barrenness or fertility. Whether it is waiting for one's period to come after a horrible sexual experience, hoping for a phone call to follow up a decent first date, or the grief of blood at a few weeks pregnant, woman after beautiful woman has confessed their longing and sorrow over dreams and hopes that they have had to bury. "Death must be mourned here. How will you as woman mourn the loss of your hope for a child?" I invite her voice and what she wants to bring to her grief and marking. She talks of having a ceremony of some type with her husband to mark the loss of hope after waiting fourteen years without getting pregnant.

Infertility is referenced as the "shriveled womb"[3] in the Bible, and I would even explain it more as a shriveled heart. The incapability of creating a child within you, if it is a desire you have, is devastating. Women and medicine have become desperate and brave by seeking alternative means such as in vitro fertilization, or IVF, in which the art of creating children becomes more about a science. I feel deep gratitude for science allowing women to get pregnant, while realizing there is a cost of co-creation with

2. Proverbs 13:12.
3. Numbers 5:21–22 (*The Message*).

God through a petri dish that is daunting at best. Pelvic floor specialists report that trauma held in the pelvic floor due to traumatic D&Cs and births is prevalent. Research states that over 90 percent of women who undergo surgeries in their abdomen will have scar tissue problems, because "the female pelvis contains a remarkable array of structures, responsible for myriad complex processes. It is situated in an area of the body that is vulnerable to injury, accessible to objects from the external environment and susceptible to infection. When structures in the pelvis heal, they can become bound by adhesions . . . causing pain and dysfunction."[4] Our wombs are sensitive and powerful, fashioned by the Creator to bear witness to the complexity of creation. Do not be fooled, the invitation to create is one of agony and glory, sometimes found in a petri dish and other times in the sacred act of intimacy. We must honor the process of healing when the womb is harmed, for it is our sanctuary made up of that which is most holy.

Miscarriage

The phone call came at the end of a long family hike near Cougar Mountain. My uncle had been put in hospice and it would be only days until he died. My sister and I flew down that weekend in hopes of saying goodbye. We left our kids home with our husbands and took a red-eye to try to catch my uncle conscious. In deep sorrow, I was able to crawl into his withering arms and speak softly our goodbyes. I whispered to him that I was pregnant and my little one would be born near his birthday. That evening before bed, there was blood when I went to the bathroom. I texted my husband but calmed him and myself as I had spotted in other pregnancies. I went to sleep and when morning came the blood hadn't stopped. We went to the ER and saw the nine-week sac only measuring six weeks and sitting low in my uterus with no heartbeat. The doctor told me there was a possibility I had the weeks wrong and we would know for certain in the next forty-eight hours. *Waiting is like no other discipline. Waiting is also like no other healer.*

The common Hebrew verb used for waiting is *yachal*, which is translated as "to have hope or be expectant" or "to remain in a state in which you expect or hope that something will happen." There is a synonymy between waiting and hoping. *Waiting cannot be attained without engaging hope.* How do you hope when you have been mocked by death? My counseling professor, Dr. Dan Allender, once said, "To the pregnant woman, she can

4. Wurn and Wurn, *Overcoming Our Infertility and Pain.*

be doing nothing but the simple act of going to the bathroom and the sight of red blood mocks her hope." There is blood. Blood is mocking my hope. At any point in a pregnancy bright red blood brings fear and anxiety. For me, I remember and repeat the words of *life* said over me during a season of death.

> *We just have to keep trying for, fighting for, hoping for life* – text from my husband, Andrew.
>
> *This is not the end.* – text from my ninety-two-year-old grandfather, Awpa.

I hold on to these words like mantras against the racing thoughts that run through my mind. I would argue this is the invitation of our Creator to create alongside. Faith and hope are some of the holiest and hardest virtues to obtain when you close the bathroom door and find that the blood has not slowed but increasingly fills the water. Faith tells you, "God is in control" and hope says "we will keep trying," but it has to be love that says aloud, "I love you sweet body and I love you sweet baby" no matter what happens. Desperate being so far from my husband and kids, but visiting my hometown, I drove straight to my grandmother's house. If I were going to miscarry this baby, I wanted to do it in her home and in her arms. Mema held me throughout the afternoon and then we had to leave for the airport. It was a long and emotionally painful plane ride back to the Northwest; the gruesome trip was only graced by my sister's gentle hand in mine. It was late into the night when we reached Seattle, and even later when I unlocked the front door to my house and tiptoed into my dark familiar bathroom. I didn't want to turn the light on, I didn't dare look how much blood had come. I sat there in the dark thinking of all the houses of relatives that I had bled in that day. My aunt's home, my dad's home, my dying uncle's home, my grandmother's home . . . and now, finally, my own home. It was time to invite the birthing process to finish and I guided my body to spill out and let go of her treasured hope, her small white sac of creation. I lit candles and then stared for such a long time at the potential life that rested there in my toilet.

When we bleed something is being shed, the potential for life or life itself is being shed and we have nothing in that moment but to stare down the invitation to mock death. I have feared death too long. Fear can only be immersed in love. I have few choices while on earth but one I do have in the face of death, is to choose to weep honorably and love deeper than I choose to fear. I weep for injustice, I weep for loss, I weep for the pain of hope, the discipline of waiting, the ache of birth and grief of death. I imagine Jesus, receiving this gift, this life, and Jesus asking to carry my small one into a heavenly womb. This intimate, sacred, painful image is my kindest, most loving thought. *My fears being drowned by perfect love.*

The next evening, I texted a few friends to meet me at our ritual spot on the shore of the Puget Sound. By moonlight we were all at the water's edge lighting candles on a rocky beach where we have met many times. We huddled in a circle keeping our candles burning and holding each other's shaking bodies. I never took my eyes off their eyes. These were the faces of the women who had been staring back at me the past five years, coaching me as I birthed my lifeless firstborn, as I birthed two years of panic attacks, as I birthed a healthy second son, as I birthed a beautiful daughter, and now as I birthed a miscarriage. Their teared and flawless eyes grounded me, and they turned me to the water. I let the icy water surround my legs, my hips, and my abdomen; I let the water baptize the womb that wept with war-torn cells. This would be my *mikveh*, the sacred cleansing ceremonial bath to restore, and this would be my way of marking with ritual my loss. Ritual will be an agent to reaching restoration, but even with this marking there is the cost of the waiting time required to heal.

Tears, Baptism, and Cleansing Research

God, our Creator, gave us tears to cleanse and baptize our bodies through the highs and lows of our lifetimes. Physiologically, there are three differ-ent types of tears: basal, reflex, and psycho-emotional tears. To stabilize your mood, the psycho-emotional tears contain stress hormones that are released so your body doesn't trap prolactin and endorphins inside, as they can become toxic to your health. These emotional tears also have natural pain killers that help you to feel better. To protect us from physical and emotional unhealth, God created our tears, our emotional *mikveh* bath to cleanse our sorrow. Research shows that women cry an average of 5.3 times a month, while men cry an average of 1.3 times per month. Women are biologically wired to shed more tears than men, since female tear glands are much smaller than men's.[5] Alex Gendler speaks about the frequency and different reasons we cry:

> Crying is so innate, we produce ten ounces per day and thirty gallons a year. Regardless of gender, we actually all cry every second of our lives and produce the same types of tears. The lacrimal gland, located in the outer part of the upper eye, is constantly secreting a protein-rich, antibacterial liquid. This fluid goes from the outer edge of the eyeball toward the cornea and lubricates the entire eye surface every time we blink. Basal tears are always in our eyes to serve the purpose of lubricating, nourishing, and protecting the eyes. The second type of tears, known as reflex tears, protect the eyes from irritants, including wind, smoke, or onions. Lastly, the third type are those that are produced by emotion. Although these tears contain higher levels of stress, such as ACTH and enkephalin —an endorphin and natural pain killer—they can also work by directly calming the iris down while signaling the emotional state to others.[6]

The baptism of tears is a function of the body to release hurt and remorse before it becomes toxic. We birth the sadness and release it, creating a baptism of tears; we come close to death in order to find rebirth and make our way to a new life again. Old church baptisms were done by putting new believers under the water almost to the point of drowning them, to signify how close to death we must come to be saved and receive a true rebirth of new life, eternal life. Jesus said in John 3, "Very truly I tell you, no one can see the kingdom of God unless they are born again." Nicodemus asked, "How can someone be born when they are old? Surely they cannot enter a second time into their mother's womb to be born!" Jesus answered, "Very truly I tell you, no one can enter the kingdom of God unless they are born of water and the Spirit. Flesh gives birth to flesh, but the Spirit gives birth to spirit. You should not be surprised at my saying, 'You must be born again.' The wind blows wherever it pleases. You hear its sound, but you cannot tell where it comes from or where it is going. So, it is with everyone born of the Spirit."

Baptism is my specialty or as my midrash team likes to joke, baptism is my favorite hobby. I have had three official church baptisms *and* at least five metaphorical baptisms. Remember, I was born not only into a Catholic culture, but to a very charismatic Catholic mother. The third-generation

5. Freedman et al., "The Interpersonal Dimension of Personality 1."
6. Gendler, "Why Do We Cry?"

baptismal dress made by my great-grandmother that I wore is the same one my children wore on their baptism days. Tradition is at the heart of the Catholic church, and that expected tradition was my first christening into a life of knowing Christ's suffering so that I might know eternal life. It wasn't long into my high school days in the Assemblies of God doctrine that I personally chose again to be baptized as a public profession of my faith. At a Sunday evening service in the baptismal tub above the altar I stated my desire to be baptized and prayed that it would lead to the baptism of speaking in tongues. My zealous soul tried so hard to concentrate on my pastor's words but I was terrified that he might drop the microphone in the water and we would be electrocuted. I do remember that I wanted to wear white but didn't want anyone to see my bra through my wet clothes, so I wore two white tank tops under my shirt. The third baptism, which took place in college, came from an anxious passion to be a radical follower of Jesus, to lay down my life and my theologies and follow him. Baptisms were wildly inspiring to my ever-rebirthing faith. These three baptisms were needed and informative in the foundation of my searching for understanding of God. These baptisms were the only way I knew to consecrate myself to God. *It was only an introduction to my true baptisms, the moments in my life when blood and pain poured out of me and death was so close it inhabited my entire abdomen, when waters broke, and I delivered a child, sometimes full of life, but more often lifeless.* Baptism comes when we break our bodies to the point where we, for a moment, carry both life and death, not knowing but believing that Christ will give us life, eternal life.

Chapter 6 Questions: God as Womb

1. What do you think about when you imagine your womb's theology? What parts of your story around your womb are particular to you and how has God found you in those places?

2. What is it that you have been asked to create? What are your womb's stories of loss, life, and death?

Re-creating After Death Exercise:

This is what I believe is being asked of every one of us. Truly, we have all walked through rites of passage where we have birthed death at some level. In some moment of our lives we thought we were birthing life and then were handed something cold and lifeless. As believers, are we being asked to create again? What is being asked of you to create again? Will you continue to attempt creating, knowing that life is not the promised result?

7

A Creating God

*Of all that is written, I love only what a person hath written with *her* blood.*
Write with blood, and thou wilt find that blood is spirit.
She *that writes in blood and proverbs doth not want to be read*
but learnt by heart.

—Friedrich Nietzsche

Co-Creating

I can feel a warm liquid quickly pouring down my cervical canal. I am fourteen weeks pregnant after a previous miscarriage. I am surprised, as I was presumed to be past the twelve-week window. I go to the bathroom to find brilliant red blood puddling. Worry is not coming like I imagined it would after the recent miscarriage. Because I had just had sex with my husband, I told myself this is probably really normal, maybe I burst some blood vessels. This does not feel like the miscarriage blood last time. I call for my husband. He is also not concerned but sad to see my fear arise. He asks how he can help. I say, "I don't want to be alone when I go to the bathroom tonight. Can I wake you up to come with me?"

We don't want to be alone in this life. We also don't want to be alone in the process of creating, and yet the process of creating human life happens solely within my body. The bleeding has stopped, and I continue my mantra that all is fine. There is little to no felt movement in the first trimester, and

79

I have loaned my Doppler out to a friend. I call my doctor's office and am kindly invited to come in and listen for a fetal heart rate. It is a midwife I have never met who checks in with me. We talk about the normalcy of bleeding after sex in early pregnancies. She helps me lie down and presses the Doppler to my abdomen. We quickly find a heartbeat that I have come to recognize is too quickly beating to be mine. Tears roll down my face in relief. "I have some trauma, well, a lot of trauma, in my birthing history, so a heartbeat is always a relieving sound." She helps me sit up and her eyes turn soft, "Your doctor filled me in on your birthing history. It is way too much for one family to bear." I thank her again and we part with deep sighs of relief.

A strong and ferocious heartbeat. That is my text to my husband.

I drive in silence, blessing my body for all of this work, praying for strength to keep going, and aware that I am alone, yet not alone. These pauses are where I find that I am invited to co-create. There is no loud cheering that I heard my child's heart beating within me just now, there is no safety of tomorrow being okay, there is only this tenuous moment where I am in the presence of co-creating with something bigger and more mysterious than myself. I keep going to the bathroom. Looking expectantly and fearfully for blood, but it hasn't come.

Relief lasts fewer than forty-eight hours before I find out that this pregnancy is also a miscarriage. I am confused by the blood, then the strong heartbeat, then the silent ultrasound. The doctor confirms that somehow I have lost the baby in the last forty-eight hours. When will my body find out there is no heartbeat, that it must grieve this baby's body out of my womb? We didn't see a heartbeat today—there was no movement in this beautiful body within me. We will go tomorrow to confirm, the dreaded walk through the hospital, the numbing emptiness inside. *Where is my faith? What is my faith? Where is my hope?*

"Christy, don't despair." She means well, but I know she has never miscarried, she has never endured a stillbirth, she has never endured birthing death. The next twenty-four hours are grueling. Sleep is hard to come by. *Toilet paper clean. Go back bed, Christy.* My head pounds, I am scared. *Where is my hope?* There is a 5 percent chance they will find a heartbeat tomorrow . . . five percent chance. *Where is my hope? God have mercy on me. Thy will be done.* I am kind to my aching body, tears slip down my cheeks as I try to return to sleep. *Jesus, I need a miracle again. And I have faith that you can do this, but Lord I have very little hope.* Faith as a mustard seed, but what of hope? How much hope do I need to move mountains?

There is no blood. There is no cramping for days. I feel stirring in my belly. I tell my subconscious mind not to hope, it is not life within. The hardest parts of these days of waiting is that I feel pregnant, and I am pregnant, but without growing life. How many times have we felt the weight of death in place that was meant for life? There are few who long to move toward suffering along with Christ. I want to be with him, but I don't want to suffer with him. I don't want to bear a cross like his; to know him more. History tells us that Christ fell three times on the way to Golgotha. I imagine what it was like to get up and keep walking. The first time he falls, what does he say? Is this my Father's will? The second time, blood is pouring out of his wounds from the physical weight of the cross, Veronica offers him the grace of a cloth, the *volto santo,* to wipe his face. The third time, agony is present, and Christ falls to the ground, Simon of Cyrene is called to carry the cross. In prayer I ask myself, do I want to really know Christ in His suffering? Do I want to carry his cross?

I feel pregnant, and my body feels clumsy in the midst of waiting through this pregnancy or miscarriage. I am holding both heartache and hope within my womb. One Sunday as I was walking into a small church, I was struck by a painting hanging in the corridor of the church. The large oil-based image was the silhouette of a pregnant woman in radiating light, with the word *hope* written across her expanded belly. What of suffering, hope? Yet, I still have a little hope, and that's okay. Hope is a part of humanity, it is a part of God and what makes us human; to kill all hope is to kill all goodness. So, I kindly wait on this womb of mine; I wait because God has invited me to know her this way.

Pregnancy History

We are sitting in a small gynecology office in southern Louisiana. I don't know anyone for miles. My husband sits next to me as I fill out the nine pages of medical forms. My pregnancy history looks like a war-torn city.

Date	Weight	Delivery	Complications
12/2011	6.7lbs.	Breech vaginal	Stillbirth
11/2012	6.2lbs.	Vaginal	None
3/2015	6.8lbs.	Vaginal	None
11/2016	8 weeks	Vaginal	Miscarriage
3/2017	15 weeks		

It is astounding to me the untracked hours and years spent by women's bodies working to create new life. How many dietary needs, waiting rooms, blood draws, immunizations, and prenatal vitamins taken? Was it in vain? The list is endless, and although we know it is worth it, are we acknowledging the war the body engages in when we produce life? These are years where only a maternal God can meet with me, a motherly God who knows what it means to have your body broken and poured out to give life to another. This is also Christ's road to Golgotha, coming to life within my own body, my own flesh broken in birth like the eucharistic bread. What an invitation to understand his suffering on the cross to offer life, eternal life. There is a deep intimacy and exhaustion found in this invitation of creating life through death.

Prepping for Surgery

There is trepidation as I prep my body for my surgery tomorrow. Dilation and curettage. Anesthesia is a kind and necessary tool at times, yet I have seen the hard work it takes to revisit the body when the mind can't remember. The body will lead you through it if you ask, but it is a disorganized and long process at times. Dormant trauma can be disorienting and painful. When the body tells us a story that the mind cannot comprehend or remember, we go through seasons of uncertainty and questioning. *Jumbled grief is disconcerting at best.* It takes a skilled surgeon of the mind to sift through the scar tissue one has developed to survive a horrific wound. So, I step into my surgery with precision and intention. Just like a good therapist, I can recognize a good doctor and care team. There is a methodical and careful process that is precisely followed. Today, my nurse was kind and thorough. She did not placate with simple phrases such as "have a good day" or "thank you so much for coming." She is careful and intentional with the disappointment and grief in the situation. She asks gentle and open-ended questions, much like I was taught to do in my first counseling classes. She prefaces with phrases like, "I know this might be hard, but what can you tell me of your prior pregnancies?" or "I had the privilege of reading your records and I know there has been previous loss—is there anything you would like to tell me in addition to the notes?" My body relaxes, and I feel cared for, my gut begins to rest, and I don't have be so vigilant about honoring myself, because I am aware she knows what it means to honor each story and each life.

Our society is intimidated around matters of death, especially infant death. The church is not much better. Heaven is our quickest answer out of the uncomfortable moment; for example, "They are in a better place." As much as that might be true theologically, it is not a response of curiosity. When someone loses something, anything: an organ, an appendage, a loved one, a pet, the other has no power to state what "it should feel like" for the one who has lost. As believers in an eternal life, we are given that hope, but we must acknowledge that "hope deferred makes the heart sick." We must settle into our discomfort with grief, or even our own experience of loss, and offer a curious and safe place for each other. We must be willing to be fools rather than cowards. This doctor did not touch the computer the entire time she was in the room, she sat next to me at my eye level. She explained the procedure and then asked if I had any questions or concerns. We talked through cremation and burial options, genetic testing, and how the baby's body is treated during and after removal. It was a painstaking but helpful conversation. I had done enough work with previous child loss that this was not a re-traumatizing situation. If there hasn't been much work in an area of loss, please be gentle and kind with yourself. Give yourself a break; sometimes ignorance or anesthesia is the kindest option until more care can happen.

Surgery Pavilion

I wanted to anoint myself this morning with oils but there are no oils allowed after the antibacterial washing. So, I look in the mirror and I say, "You are good. You are good. You are good." I allow my tears to anoint me and I dress and quickly open the door to attend to my screaming two-year-old. My mom hastily blesses me as I rush out the door. The dark sky shows a promise of dawn coming. My husband and I are frustrated and tense as we drive to the hospital. The car ride is quiet and somewhat awkward even for our eleven years of friendship. My husband is kind, but I am distant. Though this is not the time to talk about it, I say, "I think I am done with this stage of life. I have given God enough chances to give us however many children he thinks we should have." My husband doesn't respond. I know he wants more kids, and I know he respects that I have lived through five pregnancies. Yet, I feel like he has no idea what I have gone through. Even though he has been here with me through these seasons, I feel alone.

We check in for surgery, Andrew comes to the pre-op with me. I am given a gown and socks and told to take all clothes and jewelry off except for these two items. I have showered with disinfectant soap and have two small pills dissolving in either cheek. I haven't had any food or liquids. I awkwardly begin to change. I feel tired and embarrassed as my naked body is about to be stretched, opened, and carved out. I feel defeated and sad. Tears break through my veneer. This is not the way I want to be birthing, this feels humiliating and weak. Birth is such a powerful and victorious experience, yet here in this thin gown with my grippy socks I feel exposed and humiliated. I try to explain to Andrew. "Do you think this is part of the curse on women, that there will be pain in childbirth?" I had never thought about miscarriages as part of the pain for childbirth. The pain is real, it is stripping and emptying. I don't blame anyone who wants to sleep through this pain, who wants to forget and be desensitized. I don't want to mother my body in this moment, though it is scared and weak. How will I make this sacred? How will I care for my body when I want to turn away from it and not remember?

As I sleep through surgery, my husband writes these words:

Friday, March 24, 9:11 AM

I just left her. This heroine. This woman's strength and tenderness is much greater than mine. Christy my wife, I am in awe of you. Thank you, Christy. Thank you for fighting so hard for life. Your body was not meant to carry such death, yet some way, somehow it has. They just wheeled her back into surgery. To give birth, to confirm death. Again, damn it, again, birth linking arms with death. It should not be this way. It should not be. I try not to ask why; the question taunts me. God help us, is the only prayer that makes sense. We lost our sweet baby, at fifteen weeks. We thought we were out of the woods. We started to foolishly hope. I hate hope, I have to hope.

The doctor just came out and said you did great and you are just waking up. She said thirty more minutes and I can come back to be with you. I asked her if she was tender with our baby, she said yes.

Recovery

We spend the next two days in a hotel down the street from our house. I cannot feel my emotions, I feel numb and unengaged. I methodically shower and then lie back in bed. I watch show after show, trying to forget, turning my phone off to the multiple text messages. I write whenever I do feel something, but there are no tears. For more than two days, I do not cry, I do not wince when I see blood in the bathroom. I let my body move mechanically, and I avoid my reflection.

It isn't until I return to work on Monday that it comes to me. I need to ask a friend to lead a ritual to mark this baby and I need to go to see my therapist. My voice is strong and clear as I begin my session with her. "I need to go into that room, I need to be with my body as it goes through that surgery, and I need to see the baby." She is quiet, I haven't seen her in almost two years, but she hesitates, she thinks it might be too traumatizing to go to that place. One qualification of being a therapist for a decade is that you have done enough of your own work to know what you need to do, and you have some clout to tell your own therapist what you need and how to lead you. She is willing and takes me through a visualization where I walk into the surgery room and I meet my unformed little one and I hand him to Jesus. I feel his body grow warm right before I release him to an eternal world.

We finish the session and I am weeping with relief. My body relaxes into the truth. I have lost three of my five children to another world, a world where I cannot be with them. This settling truth grounds me deeper into this world that I am in. I return home and when I walk up the stairs to my front door, I can hear my children and husband inside. This time, I can really hear them. Hope reluctantly fills my lungs and I am grateful for God's kindness that I am not hardened to them or to this world. *Our tears weather the contempt in our hearts. If you really look at a person's eyes, if you take in their face, there is a map of where kindness and contempt have made their homes.* Tears baptize us.

Water the Fallow Ground

The gray sky is thick with misty rain early on this Friday morning. There is no invitation for reprieve as sunrise can't be made out on the horizon of the vast green field across our street. It is a week today since they removed our sweet baby from my womb. It is seven days since my body began bleeding to signify it realized he had been taken from us, not only his little spirit but now his small forming frame. I can hear my two children upstairs playing make believe family while putting their babies to sleep. I know I need to be present with them, I know their momma has been in fog from the last weeks of loss. I wrestle with the remaining fog over my soul and I tell God I need a little more resurrection in my life.

There are sixty plastic multicolored Easter eggs on the top of my refrigerator. Usually we would wait the two remaining weeks of Lent until we take them down to fill them. But I am desperate today, utterly desperate for some hope, for some resurrection. I take the plastic eggs down and let them spill across my white countertops. I open the cabinets and begin filling each egg with assorted morning snacks: Pirate's Booty, raisins, and cheese crackers. The kids are coming downstairs, and I tell them to close their eyes while I go hide the eggs in the front yard. My tall, green Hunter rain boots feel like armor as I set out to face the darkness of the morning, my mother heart set as flint to find hope and presence with my living children. This is the first of three Easter egg hunts we will partake in this day.

Sunday comes and it is almost silly to drive the three blocks to our church, but this morning we have little will to dry out the stroller or put on bike helmets, so we crawl into the car and arrive early. I have only told a dozen or so friends about the miscarriage, so I am forgetful how many friends still think we are pregnant. A close friend whose wife is also pregnant asks how I am feeling. I fumble through different responses until I explain we lost the baby last week. His face immediately falls, and I am uncomfortable as his tears cascade unabashedly down his cheeks. He asks if he can hug me and he holds me with a tender and discouraged grace. I let him hold me, I let my own tears collect with his on my chest. The worship music begins, and we go to our seats, the lyrics are hard to muster through my quivering voice.

Give thanks, with a grateful heart.
Give thanks to the Holy one.
Let the weak say I am strong.
Let the poor say I am rich,
Because of what the Lord has done.
Give thanks.

I am embarrassed that my body trembles every time I attempt to sing another word. I set my mind's eye on my living children's faces, trying to let the other three children stay buried in the ground. I walk to the back of the church, needing to escape the holes in my faith. My dearest friend Heather asks to take my kids after church, then she looks at me and pulls me into her arms. "Hi there, sweet one. Hi there." My tears erupt, and I am awakened to the grief of this loss in a way I have yet experienced in these past few weeks. "You are loved. You are loved. You are loved." Her whispers feel confident, like a strong and knowing mother who is not afraid to comfort my grief. She is not afraid to allow me to melt in her arms.

I walk home, the earth calling me to put my hands in dirt and work the land. I am mindful that my soul has been desperate to plant life since the miscarriage. I have been to the nursery three times this week and built garden beds and shoveled through rocks to harrow the dried soil. Yet, I must wait to plant, I must let the land lie fallow; this is my church, this is my offering of faith. I feel the sun blind me as I bury my hands deep in the empty soil, tears emerging freely, baptizing my offering of a lifeless child. I can feel my empty womb, much like these empty, seedless garden beds, is desperate and afraid to hope that something might grow here again.

Everbearing

The spring air is crisp and budding plants are hopeful for new life, yet I feel like they are mocking me. My empty womb feels plowed and harrowed but left unsown for a period of time—at this point I am not certain it will be restored its fertility. In the last year of trying to conceive, my body hasn't been able to carry a child to full term. It has been two months since my D&C procedure; this is the second miscarriage in eleven months and my body is desperate and determined to grow something that will live. I pull into the nursery parking lot and walk straight to the voluptuous display of strawberry starter plants. I want my hands to dig deep into the soil once again, so

I buy thirty starters and drive home with desperate intent. The garden beds adjacent to my house have been beautifully tilled, yet I can't come to plant anew. My exhalation sends a heavy cloud of condensation in the perfectly rounded out holes I am digging out. I have the strawberry starters lined in a row, and my nails are packed with dirt. I feel wearily alive. The small white plastic markers are covered in dirt but through it I can make out the bold black lettering: EVERBEARING. Such a hopeful and victorious word, I weep as I press the covering dirt firmly around each root. Everbearing means bearing more or less continuously. My uterus sighs a deep groaning sigh whenever I read that definition; my heart, on the other hand, perks up a little with a gleaming light. I know God invites us into the life-and-death cycle of creating. The words replay in my mind from the appointments with a genetic counselor and obstetrician specialist earlier that morning. No complications genetically, no blood pathogen complications, all looked normal. Her words don't offer much comfort, "I don't see any reason from the test results to think that a thirty-seven-year-old woman couldn't have another healthy pregnancy. Sometimes as we age our eggs aren't as good." I can feel my tears hot and pressing against my lids. It should be good news, but my uterus shrivels within me. Going over the results of our little boy's demise put me over my edge and that drove me straight to the nursery.

The heartache and beauty of an almost completed decade of my reproductive years flashes through my mind. We have had five pregnancies in almost seven years and there are only two beautiful children to show for it. If we are everbearing, all of us, we must learn to mark and make meaning of each death. So, I plant each one of those damn everbearing strawberry plants as proof that I can keep *something* alive. I rub my hands together and let the dirt fall to the ground, I turn to my house and walk into a room full of life. My children and husband are wrestling with pillows on the bed and they screech when I enter and envelop me. My husband was gentle when he asked why I had spent over $300 on plants this month. It took a while to put words to it, but I realized that I was exhausted by so much loss and death, I wanted to surround myself with living things. The Holy Spirit is speaking to our human bodies throughout the seasons, igniting desire in us to create. We as women are everbearing creatures, whether we want or don't want to have children, whether our wombs are able or not able to bear children, whether we have stories of losing children, adopting, or birthing children. *Women are everbearing creatures.* Our bodies are ever bearing the cycle of life and death, our ovaries and uterus, in particular, are ever bearing the cycle of hope and loss. These years of reproduction have not come without beauty too, and I must celebrate and honor the gratitude for the lives I have brought forth into this world.

Building a Garden

We see this cycle again and again throughout Scripture. Isaiah 5 is one of my favorite examples of this. God is singing a song about what it is like as a parent to watch His son get his heart broken in his covenant relationship with human beings.

> I will sing for the one I love
> a song about his vineyard:
> My loved one had a vineyard
> on a fertile hillside.
> He dug it up and cleared it of stones
> and planted it with the choicest vines.
> He built a watchtower in it
> and cut out a winepress as well.
> Then he looked for a crop of good grapes,
> but it yielded only bad fruit.[1]

The verse always gives me chills. It reminds me of the helpless parental heart that cannot make someone love their child; the futility a parent feels when their child gets their heart broken by a first love or a lost dream. One of my favorite worship songs is entitled "The Garden Song," which I imagine worship leader Jason Upton wrote after studying Isaiah 5:

> I want to build you a garden, in a dry and desert land, I'm going to find a river there.
> For I have seen a garden grow in a land filled with injustice
> and I have heard a mother's cry for her child to live again.
> I have seen a withered soul fall like petals on the water,
> and I watched a flower grow,
> I have seen the power of resurrection, slowly rise toward the sun.
> No one knows what God has seen,

1. Isaiah 5:1–5.

human kind destroyed this garden,
with bleeding hands, we will plant the seeds,
and You will make all things new again,
God will make all things live again.[2]

The process of creating a child is filled with awaiting hope, injustice, trauma, healing, celebration, longing, pain, and resurrection. It is much like this parable of the vineyard, which is a womb where God is trying to build a lush garden that gets destroyed because it is trying to grow in a fallen world. "The Garden Song" is a beautiful response to the brokenhearted Creator; it is a song I have tried to sing back to God in the years of my pregnancies. In the weeks of desperate waiting for a pregnancy to reach the twelve-week mark, or when I have wept with blood on my hands when my baby never made it to a viable life, I have made this my prayer. Co-creating life with God has made me a woman who has contended with faith and hope. Living through the ups and downs of a decade of reproduction, I have become a brave and wild woman who sings with faith, hope, and love. Each one of us have a birthing story, whether it is that we never had the courage to try again, never wanted to try at all, or we easily brought life into this world without struggle. Our birthing story tells us how we will come to the last stage of our lives, how we will lay down and die. I know my birth story and the story of my birthing years, and I will tell you this much: I will dance into my death like an autumn leaf falls to the ground. I ask you to study the cyclical pattern that unfolds in your menstrual story, in your birthing years; how do you come to the creation process?

Our Last Dance with the Womb

We are on the last day of our six-week, 6,000-mile road trip for the Christmas holiday. After losing two different pregnancies the day after flying, my gynecologist encourages me not to fly during this last pregnancy. It is my sixth and final pregnancy because I know my psychological state cannot handle attempting to live through another pregnancy. So, this is it, I am eleven weeks through and as nauseous as I have ever been for any pregnancy. We cancelled our flights down South and decided to drive our camper van through Oregon and California, across Arizona, New Mexico, and Texas until we made it to our destination of Louisiana. I was not going

2. Upton, "The Garden Song."

to chance a miscarriage on a plane, even if I couldn't prove that was the cause, so we drove. Had someone asked me to consider how the trip would be with a four-year-old, two-year-old, and a nauseous first trimester gut, I might not have done it. I didn't consider any of these factors, I just wanted to get to the sunshine and I was pretty desperate, so we drove for weeks there and back.

We were on a beautiful stretch home through remote northern Nevada. The mountains loomed for miles on both sides of us, our children slept quietly in the back of the van. My husband and I were talking about the new year ahead of us and what we planned personally to each take on. I had an empty bag of Goldfish crackers in my lap as a quick, makeshift throw up bag and we stared straight ahead with peppermint sticks in our mouths like cigars of tentative hope and celebration. We were trying to grow a family while building our careers and the process had done a number on us. It was silent for a long stretch after we shared our expected desires for the next year. We were comfortable with the silence and aware of our ridiculous bravery, our uncanny hope in a God who had only given us two children from our six pregnancies. We were resolved to try this last pregnancy, knowing my psyche and body could not take another attempt after this one. So, in a sense, holding our breath as we waited, we drove cross country instead of flying, not sure that would change anything. It seemed as if we were stating our faith to God that we would persevere again in blind hope that there would be a miracle and this child would live. Our repeated action was continued hope for life to come from desolate places of death, and to honor and cherish those places of bravery that were once beautiful naive dreams.

We have a choice to respond to our Creator, whose heart is beating more loudly and wildly than ours to continue to bring life to death. The cycle of the womb invites us again and again to participate in the co-creation of bringing life where there was death. We recognize that the co-creating years with God are some of the most straining times in a marriage, with our partner and with the God we serve. We are trying to co-create as faithfully as we can, to build a family, a garden, a legacy that evil has tried to thwart but we have our face set as flint against the odds. We are waiting for a God who makes all things *live* again.

Postpartum

Pieces of grilled cheese are falling into my newborn's hair, along with my continuous tears that now have soaked a huge portion of his sleep sack. I am holding my baby in the infamous football hold, doing squats so low my thighs are screaming almost as loudly as the whooshing noise I am making right in his ear. I can hear my kids in the other room practically raising themselves because the torture of sleep deprivation has taken their mother away from them. I am desperate to find God somewhere in this season of my life. Actually, I probably couldn't care less about anything but sleep. I have to wonder what God looks like during postpartum. I wonder if he almost lost his mind trying to get us to calm down and sleep through the night. I think that God, like a mother, is trying desperately at seasons of our lives, to get us to rest and to trust him. My belief is that God is longing for us to live securely attached to him. Yet depression and seasonal affective disorder are the most common diagnoses I work with in my practice. The fight to live through postpartum depression is a real battle and one that we need community to help us live through.

Postpartum refers to the period of time for the mother after the birth and the postnatal care of the baby. It involves the sharp drop in the hormones progesterone and estrogen, which contribute to feeling tired, depressed, and sluggish. Postpartum, in particular postpartum grief, is only recently being addressed in the medical world. Medical experts report that a woman's body needs two years to fully recover from childbirth. The range of emotions in a woman after childbirth oscillates between joyful attachment and bliss to protective nightmares and panic-ridden anxiety. The mother's brain shifts and we see changes in the prefrontal cortex, amygdala, and all the regions of the brain that control empathy, social interactions, and anxiety. When a woman is in recovery from miscarriage or birth, one must be aware that it is hard to explain what is happening in the brain and the healing process of postpartum. It is helpful to engage anyone in a season of postpartum with curiosity and care through this transition period.

Birthing Life and Death

Birthing life and birthing death have many similarities. In fact, as women, our wombs become the great teachers of birthing life and death. Sage

Femme. This is the term given usually to midwives who have studied the art of birthing. Sage Femme means wise woman. If we follow the instruction of our cycle, the womb teaches us the ways of birthing. There are two kinds of births, one with a capital "B" and the other with a lowercase "b." Ever since my kids were Birthed, I have had to birth almost daily. Birthing life with a capital B is what we refer to most commonly when we speak of childbirth. Yet, as humans, we birth things every day, in every interaction we engage. A fully alive human births life with a lowercase "b" everywhere they go. It is the act of creating.

There is a wedding sermon I teach often when I marry couples. I explain to the crowd that a marriage soul is born the moment these two people vow to create a life. This birth is a soul that exists outside of them but is made up of them. A marriage soul is much like a child. Every couple who enters into a marriage covenant births a life into this world and it is named Marriage. These lowercase "b" births don't have to be as extravagant as a wedding; it can be as simple as trying to leave the house. What I mean by this is that there isn't a day when my husband and I don't feel the birthing pains of trying to get the kids dressed and out the door to go somewhere. Each of our days as humans are full of births and deaths and we feel them inside of our bodies as we are invited to co-create in this life with God. The counter is true of this concept, we can also birth capital "D" Death or lower case "d" death into this world. Death with a capital "D" is obviously defined as the human body shutting down and the soul leaving this world. If we take the idea of birthing death, we see there is an art to birthing and a way to allow death to be birthed well. What do I mean by this? There are many opportunities to birth deaths, and they are also invitations from our Creator to suffer with him. Lower case "d" deaths can be anything from the death of a dream, getting fired from a job, selling a home, failing an exam, getting a divorce, or moving to a new city. Our God, the Creator of the universe, invites all of us into the process of creating through birthing life and death.

Death and grief have many symbolic similarities to birth, and in many ways, we give birth to death. The aftermath of death, the burial process, for me has looked a lot like postpartum grief. Postpartum is different for everyone, and I think the same is true with postpartum grief. Often after one has a baby we ask the question, "How was the birth?" The same is appropriate for the postpartum griever; we should ask, "How was the death?" Whether death is difficult and painful or worthy of the celebration of reaching eternal life is dependent on the details of the death, much like the details of a birth. How did one come to die? Were they sick or in pain? Was there family nearby? Did they get to say goodbye to everyone they desired, or were they taken too quickly? Was it accidental, intentional; timely, expected? These answers don't tell us whether one should grieve more or less around this death, rather it gives us details of how the person grieving might encounter the next few months of postpartum grief. Trauma happens when death comes outside of the proper order. Death has a specific place in time and when that time line is breached, death can be traumatic. We must be curious of the grieving process as we are of the birthing process.

Chapter 7 Questions: A Creating God

1. Where has God invited you to co-create with him?

2. What have you birthed?

3. What are the birth stories of your pregnancies?

4. What has postpartum been like for you? How do you come to grieve and bless the wear on your body it takes to create?

8

God as Mother

Again, and again, motherhood demands that
we break through our limitations,
that we split our hearts open to make room
for something that may be more than we thought we could bear.
In that sense, the labor with which we give birth is simply a rehearsal for
something we mothers must do over and over: turn ourselves inside out
and then let go.

—SUSAN PIVERS, *The Mindful Way through Pregnancy*

God in the Kitchen

THE FAMILIAR BLUE AND white wallpapered kitchen awakens slowly each lazy weekend morning as my grandpa drinks his coffee and my grandma sips her Diet Dr. Pepper, while they rock quietly in their matching rocking chairs. They slowly greet the morning. Soon the creaking silence will be interrupted as kids, grandkids, and great-grandkids start drifting in to say good morning and begin the cooking. The daylight hours are filled with the men barbecuing while playing with the kids outside in the backyard, and the women congregating with the babies in the kitchen. No one dares start the family secret recipe marinara sauce until Aunt Dee arrives, as no one can make eggplant Parmesan like she can. Otherwise, chopping and chattering fill the room like a seamless melody. My grandma and nanny usually sit in the rocking chairs with a baby in each arm while my sisters and cousins help our mommas on side dishes. There is nothing we don't talk about, and when my Aunt Linda is visiting, there is no question not allowed. The morning melts into the afternoon without question of needing to be anywhere else. The smell of eggplant Parmesan has permeated our clothes by the time the meal is finally ready to be served and eaten. We never eat our very Italian, Saturday afternoon meals before 2 PM. I wouldn't have known to name it anything other than family dinner; yet now I would identify it as a ritual of sorts, being amongst my mothers. My great-grandmother, grandmother, mother, great aunts, aunts, sisters, and cousins gathered in the kitchen cooking a weekend meal.

Yolanda Pierce, a theology professor at Princeton Theological Seminary, was published in the *New York Times* with this example of what God being Mother means to her:

> Long before I became familiar with the academic debates concerning calling God "Mother," debates that I am now currently a part of as a professor at Princeton Theological Seminary, I was being raised in a household where I instinctively understood that the divine presence was manifest in the loving hands and arms of mothers, and most especially in the life of my grandmother who raised me. My grandmother's kitchen was a theological laboratory where she taught me how to love people just as naturally as she taught me to make peach cobbler and buttermilk biscuits. I watched and listened as she ministered to the sick and the lost, with a Bible in one hand and a freshly baked pound cake in the other, despite having no official ministry role.
>
> I knew that if God was real, if God truly loved me as a parent loves a child, then God was also "Mother" and not only "Father." Only years of dogma and doctrine force you to unlearn what you know to be true in your own heart, demanding "Father" as the only acceptable appellation and concept for God.[1]

God has been female, woman, and mother to many for a long time. Many people don't know this, but God references herself as woman many times in the Bible:

1. Deuteronomy 32:11–12, God described as a mother eagle, "Like the eagle that stirs up its nest, and hovers over its young, God spreads wings to catch you, and carries you on her wings."

---

1. Pierce, "Why God Is a 'Mother,' Too."

2. Deuteronomy 32:18, God who gives birth, "You were unmindful of the Rock that bore you; you forgot the God who gave you birth."

3. Psalm 22:8–10, God as a midwife, "'He trusts in the Lord,' they say, 'let the Lord rescue him. Let him deliver him, since he delights in him.' Yet you brought me out of the womb; you made me trust in you, even at my mother's breast. From birth I was cast on you; from my mother's womb you have been my God."

4. Psalm 123:2–3, God as mistress, "As the eyes of a servant looks to the hand of their master, as the eyes of a maid to the hand of her mistress, so our eyes look to you, YHWH, until you show us your mercy!"

5. Psalm 131: 2, God as one who weans, "But I have calmed and quieted myself, I am like a weaned child with its mother; like a weaned child I am content."

6. Matthew 23:37 and Luke 13:34, God as a Mother Hen, "Jerusalem, Jerusalem, the city that kills the prophets and stones those who are sent to it! How often have I desired to gather your children together as a hen gathers her brood under her wings, and you were not willing!"

7. Ezekiel 19:2, God as lioness, "What a lioness was your mother among the lions! She lay down among them and reared her cubs."

8. Job 38:29, God who gives birth, "Who is the mother of the ice? or From whose womb comes the ice? Who gives birth to the frost from the heavens?"

9. Hosea 11:3–4, God described as a mother God, "Yet it was I who taught Ephraim to walk, I who took them up in my arms; but they did not know that I healed them. I led them with cords of human kindness, with bands of love. I was to them like those who lift infants to their cheeks. I bent down to them and fed them."

10. Hosea 13:8, God described as a mother bear, "Like a bear robbed of her cubs, I will attack them and tear them asunder."

11. Numbers 11:12, God as a conceiving and nursing mother, "Did I conceive all these people? Did I give them birth? Why do you tell me to carry them in my arms, as a nurse carries an infant, to the land you promised on oath to their ancestors?"

12. Isaiah 42:14, God as a woman in labor, "For a long time I have held my peace, I have kept myself still and restrained myself; now I will cry out like a woman in labor, I will gasp and pant."

13. Isaiah 49:15 and 1 Thessalonians 2:7, God as a nursing mother, "Can a mother forget the baby at her breast and have no compassion on the child she has borne? Though she may forget, I will not forget you!"

14. Isaiah 66:13, God as a comforting mother, "As a mother comforts her child, so I will comfort you; you shall be comforted in Jerusalem."

God is naming herself: woman, mistress, breast, conceiver, womb, pregnant, birth, postpartum, nursing, mother eagle, mother bear, hen, and lioness. I will not talk about each of these verses in detail, but take in how often God uses the woman's attributes to explain who God is.

Manger Theology

I remember the first time I heard Nikki Giovanni interviewed by Krista Tippett. I was a young mother of two kids taking a rare flight back home. My husband had been keeping the kids for the weekend and I was listening to a podcast, which I hadn't done since before my last baby was born. I remember feverishly writing down as many notes as I could as I listened to the interview. I was captivated by the concept of a manger theology.[2] Tears came to my eyes when I heard a woman talk about how, as Christians, we look to the cross all the time, yet don't equally look to the birth in the manger. I was stunned at her words, because I had thought of that so many times when I was in the birthing room or lighting my Advent candles preparing for Christ's birth. Because we hesitate to over-glorify Mary, we fail to grasp the theological significance of the birth of Christ with as much fervor as we do the death of Christ. This idea sparked something in me, something that I had been thinking and feeling for a long time. My aloneness in the birthing process and pregnancies was where I needed to start looking to understand God. All this time, I had been looking to friends who were pregnant at the same time for companionship, or a mothers group that could understand what I was going through and help me wade through these waters of loneliness. It was really hard to find God during that season, and yet what I knew but couldn't yet articulate was that I felt God right there, so intimately growing a child in my womb. My journey of motherhood did not connect very easily with my church experience and sermons from the pulpit. I wanted to learn about the motherhood of God because I felt God in my motherhood. I didn't know how to articulate it then, and I

2. Tippett, "Soul, Food, Sex and Space."

didn't know how to connect with God fully, yet I came to realize God was there every time I went to the bathroom, every time I've looked in the mirror at my expanding belly, and every time I felt a kick of an alien inside of me. I felt intimate with God not as a man, but with all the feminine qualities of God, the femaleness of God.

The manger story is about the greatest birth, the birth of our Savior. The manger story is also about women's collective story to be creators. Manger theology includes the holy gift of the womb placed inside a woman's body, which is created to birth life. It is the woman's body that is invited to break open to learn the ways of our Creator. The birthing room is a place where there was never meant to be pain, only glory, until sin came into the world and God cursed creating with pain. Genesis 3:16 is the infamous curse that leaves women to toil with the pain of childbirth. Women from this moment on carry the glory of creation alongside the pain from the curse inside their bodies. We bear the magnificence of co-creating life with God while we also bear with God the suffering of enmity between a parent and their offspring.

Snakes and Dreams

Snakes like two things, warmth and water. I hate snakes. Growing up in the Deep South, I spent my childhood killing a lot of snakes. Tromping through uncharted woods around a man-made lake quickly taught me to distinguish a water moccasin from a garden snake. Those damn water moccasins would open their mouths wide before an attack, revealing the poison filled cotton-looking sacs on their glands and scaring the living tar out of me. Yet over time, I learned how to kill them. Whether it was with a large rock, a machete, or a BB gun, I could pretty quickly kill the predator and remove and bury the head (where the poison was held) before tying its long body around to the edge of the ATV grill to practice skinning later. I tried to act cool around guys when it came to snakes; I didn't want to be "that girl" who was freaked out by them. My boyfriend in college had a pet snake, which I actually allowed to take naps around my shoulders for hours. But as I age, I am more honest, and I can't stand snakes. Snakes expose my vulnerability, and snakes, not only biblically, remind me of sheer evil.

Interestingly, women are given authority over snakes (i.e., evil) in Scripture. My precious Catholic mother has had many statues in her life, but there is one that I will never forget. On her kitchen window sill, directly in front of the sink, there is a statue of Mother Mary standing with her arms open surrender-like, and under her feet is a snake she has killed. The image is etched deeply in my mind, a woman so meekly asserting death over this creature by crushing it under her feet. In the Bible, the snake represents the personification of the self-accusing conscience. In Genesis 3:15 (NIV), there are concepts to note: *enmity* is set between the woman and her seed. Now, *seed*, a word usually used for a man, here refers to the woman's descendants. And that snake is there again, to bruise the heel of woman's descendants and in response, the woman crushes the head of the snake. However, you instead might interpret that, enmity (i.e., hate) is illustrated through a snake attacking a woman's creation and in response, she kills the snake. *The woman has authority to kill the snake.*

It is fairly common for me to have the same recurring dreams about snakes. In most nightmares they have slithered into my son's attic loft bedroom and are about to bite his sleeping body. On a handful of nights, I sleepily make my way up the stairs and survey his room and bed for any slithering creatures. What is this dream of my boy's sleep being interrupted by an evil, biting snake? The verse comes to mind, "the snake will bruise the heel of the woman's seed"[3]; is my little boy not my seed? Although there could be a myriad of interpretations I could share with you, this is what I have found. The nights I dream of snakes, I usually am in a vulnerable state (e.g., going through a miscarriage, afraid of death, panic attacks, or pregnant). When we are vulnerable in attempting to create life, the process of death as part of that creation can easily haunt us by evil making us fear.

This dynamic can show up in so many places for a woman when it comes to her seed. I have seen evil bruise the heel of Eve's creation, whether it is through rampant isolation and depression, domestic violence, rape, divorce, infertility, lack of creativity, loss of job or passion, miscarriages, death of family or friends, dryness in their spiritual lives, grief of stillbirth, or the loss of desire. There are too many to list. Death clearly has never been from God, and women are given authority to crush that snake with our heel. Women were given this power to crush this snake of evil when it attacked "her seed", i.e. her creativity, her ability to create. I am not speaking only of physical children, I see her descendants as anything she creates with her body: a smile, an orgasm, a hug, a legacy of things that come to life from her body. Can we overcome death? Debatable in the physical sense, but we clearly have been given power to crush its head. When we create anything life-giving, we overcome death. As I explained earlier, the head of the snake

3. Genesis 3:15 (NIV).

is where the poison and the bite lie. To crush the head is to give women biblical authority to protect and nurture their seed, their life-giving attributes. It also identifies that woman's seed, woman's descendants (e.g., her spirituality, creativity, arts, children, legacy, sexuality) will be at risk of evil preying on her whenever she is in the midst of creating something alive.

How does evil attack your life-giving abilities? Be aware that dreams often help us explore these ideas. If you haven't in the past, start tracking your dreams. This is an easy way to begin to awaken the wild feminine. Your dream world, though often not literal, is very alive and explanatory of what is going on in the subconsciousness of your life. If you don't regularly dream, become aware of your sleep, and dreams will come if you allow them. The wilderness in you wants to be allowed to grow, and dreams are a great place to start to awaken because you actually get to sleep while doing it![4]

God as Mother Bear

"Like a bear robbed of her cubs,
I will attack them and tear them asunder . . ."

—HOSEA 13:8 (GOD DESCRIBED AS A MOTHER BEAR)

Every year in late August, you can find my family and me tubing down Icicle River. The warm sun beats down on my skin, the chilly water awakening me to the adventure. For almost a decade, eight families have gathered for a long weekend in the large cabin at the edge of the river. It is not uncommon to see different groups of kids and adults taking turns tubing around the peninsula. My friend Heather and I decided to take our little girls for a special rite-of-passage-like tube ride. Their three-year-old bodies were giddy with nervous excitement, as it was known that we might see bears crossing the river along the way. I had my three-month-old son strapped to me on our inner tube, and Heather had the older girls secured in an inner tube next to her. We set off, five adventurous warriors on a bear hunt down the river. Little did Heather and I know that we would find more adventure than we'd bargained for. We stopped to play at Sandcastle Island, letting the girls dig their hands deep in the sand for a while. Then, we jumped

4. Towns, *My Father's Names*.

back into our inner tubes and continued down the river, watching four deer cross just behind us. The girls squealed with delight. Nearly back to the cabin, we spotted a small bear cub on the beach shore ahead, within twenty feet of us. Heather made quick eye contact with me as we paddled more intentionally to the opposite shore. We were both looking desperately for the mother bear, because we both knew that a mother bear would be close by and more likely to attack if we neared her young cub. We also knew that we were no match for a momma bear. The girls were wild with excitement, as they couldn't wait to get closer to the cub. I felt as helpless as a mother could, with my three-month-old baby boy in my arms and my three-year-old daughter floating nearby. Heather grabbed six smooth, large rocks and handed one to each little girl. She took two for herself and handed me two. It seemed Heather was taking notes from David and Goliath, and I chuckled a little when we told the girls to hold on to their beloved rocks and only use them if needed. We made our way past the beach shore as loudly as we could manage, and we kept as much distance as we could from the occupied land. Our eyes were fixed intently on the cub playing close by. After we had passed safely, we spotted the mother bear eating in the bushes a little farther from the shore. We immediately relaxed once could see the mother bear was safely behind us, and eagerly observed her grazing from a farther distance.

It took me a long time to become aware of the term *mother bear* and recognize how it resonates with feminine tendencies. When I did hear of the concept, I realized it was happening within me long before I became a mother in the physical sense. It is an instinct rising within which is unstoppable; a force that must be addressed. It comes when we love something so deeply that we rage to defend it from being harmed. Barring any physical limitations, we rise up and respond. The births of my children, however, did help me to recognize the feeling more acutely.

Becoming a mom is a rite of passage. Somehow, the process of birth teaches you the mechanics of an act you will continue to do with your children. My daughter took a seven-day trip with her daddy to the East Coast this year. We didn't really think that she would mind being away from me, but her tear-filled saucer brown eyes every night over the video call told me otherwise. She caught a cold while she was away, so, naturally, I was an anxious wreck being away from her. My husband tried his best, but his efforts were a small comfort for her mother-seeking heart. Our sweet family friends were housing them, and my friend Nicole knew exactly what to do.

She is a mother of four incredible girls, and my heart rested knowing she would be with my daughter. My anxiety is often calm when I know there is another mother who is with my children. My mom often makes these two statements: "There is nothing like a woman, she is worth her weight in gold" and "The hand that rocks the cradle rules the nation." It isn't until I need someone to help me that I realize her statements are extremely true. If I want something done, I ask a woman; and if it has to do with my kids, I ask a momma. The entire verse in Hosea 13:8 reads, "Like a bear whose cubs have been taken away, I will tear out your heart. I will devour you like a hungry lioness and mangle you like a wild animal."

I can vouch for this kind of *devouring* that a mother can do. God did not use male animals to illustrate God's rage—God used female animals to explain how angry and upset she felt. I have actually been closer to a lioness than I ever wanted to be in my life. My husband and I were on a night safari in Africa when our guide shined a spotlight on a lioness who was ravaging an antelope with her young. She was teaching her three cubs how to kill, tear, and eat the animal for their own survival. I was in awe watching this female creature devour this antelope, and in front of her children. The guide went on to tell us that the lioness only has two years to teach her cubs how to survive before she is pregnant again and her cubs must leave her. Roughly half of the cubs live through the first two to three weeks after they leave their mothers. A lioness' greatest job is to teach her young to survive, she is the lifeline that tells them how to navigate this world. My kids are only allowed to watch *Mr. Roger's Neighborhood*. I can't fathom teaching them to kill and rip apart a creature.

God as a Comforting Mother

"As a mother comforts her child, so I will comfort you;
you shall be comforted in Jerusalem."

—ISAIAH 66:13 (GOD AS A COMFORTING MOTHER)

The Webster's Dictionary defines *mother* as a noun meaning "a female parent; woman holding a responsible position similar to that of a mother; a creative source; qualities attributed to a mother, such as capacity to love; to give birth to; be the mother of; to create, produce; to watch over, nourish, and protect; to act or serve as a mother." The Mother-like God who carries us in her womb, who births us, nurses us, and then must wean us is a God who is comforter, remember—the Hebrew meaning for womb. Isaiah 66 reads: "Thus, says the Lord, I will nurse you, extending you peace, I will comfort you like you were within my womb." For me, it seems easier to know God as Savior, husband, maybe the one who judges or rules. May we be comforted by God, *El Shaddai*, the strong One who is able to deliver, and the tender One who nourishes us as a mother nurtures her child at her breast.[5]

Maybe it is a gut response, but more than that, it feels instinctual: when it comes to her children's well-being, a mother would give not only her life but all that is comfortable to provide for her child, the one she brought into this world. This seems like God to me; I want to believe in this type of love and mothering way. This ancient mothering impulse, a divine instinct, comforting and compassionate, translates in Hebrew Scripture as *racham*, meaning "womb." As I lay there holding my own sick child, pondering this idea of Mother God, El Shaddai, our God began to mother me, to tell me that she would comfort me, would help me sleep, would stay awake and watch over me. I knew that when I awoke, El Shaddai would nourish me just as I would do for my own baby.

God, Our Mother, Is Always Awake

It's 3:18 AM
The sweat from his head is wet on my chest.
His breathing is labored, and he won't nurse because he is so congested.
I hold a bottle of my milk warmed and he drinks a little.
If I lay him down, he cries, so, with pillows tucked around me like a throne, I sit up with his small twenty-pound frame resting against my own engorged breast.

I haven't acknowledged my exhaustion, although it has been a very long week of sleepless nights, as it is for most parents when a little one is sick. There is no margin for being tired tonight, I am mother.
One thinks of many things during sleepless nights,
I watched the dark sky and stars outside our bedroom window.
I think about countless things.
I did what a mother should do for their sick child.

5. Towns, *My Father's Names*, 43.

I stayed awake while the world slept.
I think that is a motherly attribute about God.
God does not slumber, God does not sleep. God watches over.
This mother-like God reminded me of her sleepless care over me.

God as Nursing Mother

God: "Can a woman forget her nursing child, or show no
compassion for the child of her womb? Even these may forget, yet I
will not forget you."

—ISAIAH 49:15 (GOD COMPARED TO A NURSING MOTHER)

I am not as anxious with my daughter Selah as I was during the first year
of my boy Wilder's life. Selah is like a tank of a little girl, she is healthy
and strong. And I have lived through two life-giving births, so it seems my
hippocampus is resting more than usual. The first time Selah bit my nipple
while nursing, it took everything in me not flick her little cheek with my
fingers. Instead, I screamed, and watched as the blood from my bleeding
nipple did not stop her from drinking my breast milk. I watched as she
continued to suckle my breast in pursuit of a faster flow of milk. She is
ravenously demanding, and I love her for it. I somewhat teasingly say to
her, "How could a mother ever forget you nursing at her breast?" I speak a
blessing over her, "The Lord will not forget you, Selah."

When God takes on the naming of himself, everyone stops to listen.
He doesn't waste his time giving himself names that don't matter; rather, his
names hold deep currents of reverberating truth in them. God tells stories
and we remember them. We find ourselves reflecting on them when we are
alone or driving home or sitting in traffic: "*Even if a nursing mother forgets
you, I will not forget you.*"[6] That isn't a simple promise.

If you have had a successful experience nursing a child, you can
vouch for the fact that it is a long, literal pouring out of oneself. Whether
it is squeezing out colostrum those first days at the hospital, the process of
learning the proper latch once your milk comes in, round the clock feed-
ings, or pumping in a bathroom stall on a work break or in an airport, the
life of a nursing mother is not for the faint of heart. When my husband and

6. Isaiah 49:15 (NIV).

I discuss the idea of having another child, we always ask ourselves: can our marriage handle another three-year blow; a year of being pregnant, the first year of life, and the last breastfeeding year where my sex drive is pretty low. We have learned not to discount that last year, when I am still anchored to the baby through breastfeeding and our intimacy is still making a come-back. When God says it is hard for a mother to forget the child at her breast, he isn't lying. Yet he goes further, "Even if she forgets you, I will not." God is basically saying, "*Child, you and I will always have a secure attachment, whether or not you have that with your biological mother.*"

As therapist and theologian, I am fascinated when I ponder our rela-tionship to God within the context of psychology. As a therapist who uses attachment and attunement to God as a huge part of my practice, it felt only natural to connect attachment theory to the concept of God as mother with her children. The history of attachment theory began immediately after World War II, when psychoanalyst John Bowlby was asked by the United Nations to write a pamphlet on the issue of homelessness and or-phaned children, as this was a large demographic within a war-recovering society. Maternal deprivation was the subject of his pamphlet, in which he addressed the impact of those now deprived and starving emotionally for a mother. John Bowlby is now known as the father of attachment styles, which he describes as the lasting psychological connectedness between human beings. Attachment theory in a nutshell explains how much the parents' relationship with their child influences development and a child's style of relating to the world. So, as we explore the three most common attachment styles, I want you to ask yourself how you relate to the mother in God within these categories. How have you attached to your own mother and ultimately, how have you attached to God as a parent?

The three main attachment styles:

- *Secure/Autonomous Attachment*: children have more basic trust; more resiliency, can cope with setbacks and recover more quickly.

- *Avoidant/Dismissive Attachment*: carry anger and anxiety uncon-sciously; build defenses against perceiving emotional information; displaced aggression and more non-compliance.

- *Ambivalent/Preoccupied Attachment*: no room for having a mind of one's own; have difficulty regulating the expression of negative emotions.[7]

7. Bowlby, *Attachment*.

Usually, when it comes to attachment, *we are not receptive to what we have not been given.* An insecure attachment feels chaotic and predisposes you to prefer chaos in relational dynamics. Healthy attachment is trust in our own body as you engage the world, while evil is constantly working to create betrayal. Again, it must be understood that how we attach to our primary caregiver is often the lens through which we see God and come to understand his love. What is most true is that *no matter what kind of attachment style you have with your parents,* God is waiting to offer you a secure and constant love.

God as a Mother Who Weans

"But I have calmed and quieted my soul, like a weaned child with its mother; my soul is like the weaned child that is with me."

—PSALM 131:2 (GOD AS A MOTHER WHO WEANS)

My kids are fierce in their nursing. Luckily, I have had a minimal share of bleeding nipples and being bitten, but my children love their "momma milk." Comfort is an innate desire for all of us when vulnerable or hurt. Weaning is prefaced by the belief that our kids no longer need our milk or our sustenance, that they can survive on their own. Because attachment is a huge part of my work with clients, I always am curious about how a client was weaned. How a mother lets go of her child is telling; how she sends the child away from her reveals in what way she trusts the bigger story, and her God. Although the egg is fertilized with a man's sperm, the baby grows inside of us from God's mastery. When a woman births a child through her body, she takes ownership of a child and works to sustain that child with her body for the next year or so. Through the act of breastfeeding, we literally pour our body into our child's.

> For thus says the Lord: "Behold, I will extend peace to her like a river, and the glory of the nations like an overflowing stream; and you shall nurse, you shall be carried upon her hip, and bounced upon her knees. As one whom his mother comforts, so I will comfort you; you shall be comforted in Jerusalem."[8]

How we attach and how loved we feel by our parent God speaks to how we interact with others in our faith. How we attach is connected with

8. Isaiah 66:12–13 (NIV).

how we were *weaned*. Somewhere between four to six months old, a baby begins to understand that his mother's body is no longer attached to his own. Weaning is the process of gradually introducing a mammal infant to what will be its adult diet and withdrawing the supply of its mother's milk. This is a mother's job, to teach our children how to soothe themselves. We must teach our children that they are okay, even apart from their mother.

My favorite version of the Psalms reads, "Surely, I have calmed and quieted my soul; like a weaned child with his mother, like a weaned child is my soul within me [ceased from fretting]." *To cease from fretting.* The child is not only weaned but is laying at its mother's breast calmed and not fretting at not have the mother's milk; not needing the mother for sustenance, only comfort. Charles Spurgeon comments,

> That is a very blessed thing to be able to do, to quiet yourself when, like a weaned child, you are crying under the afflicting hand of God, when you feel a proud spirit murmuring, and want to understand what cannot be understood, and you worry because you are not omniscient. Oh, it is a blessed thing, then, to say to yourself, "Be quiet, child! Be quiet!" What art thou but a child, after all, at best? What do you know? What can you know? Art you not satisfied to hear thy Father say, "What you knowest not now, thou shalt know later?"[9]

I was disturbed by Spurgeon's response, his brashness in saying "Be quiet child, Be quiet!" and then in my discouraged state, I came across these words by Alexander Maclaren:

> It is not the tranquility of a calm nature which speaks here, but that the speaker has entered by the vigorous MASTERY of disturbing elements. How hard the struggle has been and how much bitter crying and petulant resistance there had been before the calm was won, is told by the lovely image of the weaned child.[10]

I really think this beautifully states the wrestling the child has endured to wean and come to a place of peace. There is a process here, first the vigorous mastery of disturbing elements, then sadness, being withheld from, frustration, longing unmet that moves to calm and un-fretting because of the mother's assurance that the child is okay and will survive on its own. The mother's role goes from sustenance to comfort. I have known and know

9. Spurgeon, *The Treasury of David,* 116.
10. Maclaren, *Bible Class Expositions,* vol. 17, 342.

this frustration with God, this wrestling in my own faith with wanting what I am no longer allowed to have or understand. So, as we listen to Maclaren describe the child's experience with the struggle of weaning, I resonate with the wrestling of disturbing elements and then long for the un-fretting calm and comfort.

I want to talk about the mother's experience of weaning—my experience, which is possibly something similar to the Mother in God and how she feels towards her children as they wean. This verse comes to me very differently. I would never tell my child to be quiet, don't tell my child to quiet what is their worst fear, their greatest battle at this point in life, which is to face feeling alone . . . to face learning that their life source is separate from them, and they are trying to survive in this world. Anything that would harm them, I would lay down my life to save them from it. I am a fierce mother; I am not afraid when it comes to defending my children. My protection is fierce. I believe our God would do no less for her children. A mother God comforts, defends, and nourishes. She teaches her children they are safe and loved. This fierce love forms a secure attachment. When we understand that where we come from is stable and we are loved, even if we can't explain it, even if we don't like it, we still find a way to rest on our Creator's chest no longer with tears or fretful breathing, but calm.

The Gift of the Father, to Be Mother

"I love you more."

"No, I love *you* more."

This game can go on for fifteen minutes at least before bedtime in our home. If my five-year-old ever gets stuck, he knows how to "beat" me at this game. "Jesus loves me more than you do, Momma." I always start to contest and then have to stop. Although it doesn't feel possible, I attempt to believe it is true. The concept always demands me to stop and ponder. I concede and tonight explain a little more in depth. "Well, you were God's son first, and then he gave you to us, and we are so thankful he did! You are one of our greatest gifts." We are taking the stairs slowly up to his room when he turns and says, "Actually, Mom, you are the one who had me first in your belly and gave me to our family, so you really gave the greatest gift." I kiss him goodnight and finish our bedtime routine before I sit with his words. How kind for my five-year-old to bless my body, my womb, for giving our family the gift of children. And how is it that God was kind enough to invite me into the process of birthing life into this world? How did I get blessed with the gift of carrying a child within me that becomes a soul in this world?

The gift of the Father, to be mother.

Belly Buttons

My newborn baby is passed out, milk-drunk on the bed in the summer heat. This high temperature has us all wilting, so I take my little girl in the room with another fan and lay next to her for a rest time. I pull up my shirt to let the fan cool me down. She puts her finger in my belly button and asks me if that's where she came out of my belly. Her questions keep coming and she asks if it tore my bones when she was born. I laugh and say no, explaining that it only tore my skin. She responds, "Can I see it?" I tell her that it was all sewn up, but then she notices the fresh stitches across my lower abdomen and asks if she can touch them. Her questions relentless, she wants to know if I could open up the stitches so that she can see what's inside. I tell her no, I couldn't do that, but her curiosity is beautiful. I love her little finger now tracing the line of my C-section cut sutured just six weeks ago.

I want to be a safe place for my daughter's questions, I want her to feel comfortable with her feminine body. I will teach her to not fear the ignorance of birth and babies. Because maybe it's all too much for her small little brain to take in, she takes her finger and traces it up to my belly button, which in my family we call "the momma spot." I always kiss my children on their belly buttons and tell them if they ever miss me they can touch their belly button and be connected to me magically, because that's where they were connected to me before they were born. The "momma spot" is a link that we will always have. The belly button is the mark that tells them they came from somewhere and they belong. The belly button is the reminder of the lifeline that was cut and tied by their daddy after I birthed them into this world. My kids are fascinated that at one point they belonged to my body, and now they have their own personal body. Should they ever forget, they can remind themselves they belong, and they come from a mother. In this way, I needed to find God after the stories of my pregnancies and in many ways, I needed to know that I come from a Mother. I found my faith coming back differently after birth, death, and trauma. When it had become triggering and hard for me to worship, when I understood God through my own mothering heart, I began to sing again, a song from the womb. Worship and communion were often met with my tears or my silence. In many ways, I had to spiritually, and sometimes physically, touch my own belly button and remember where I came from. I needed ask if I could trace mother God's abdomen and find her belly button, to tell myself that I belonged to her and God was my great Mother. So, as I find comfort in the attributes of God, the belly button is the scar story in which I ground myself in God's love, just as my children can touch their belly buttons and ground themselves in my love.

Are you made in the *imago Dei*? If you are made in the image of God, your God encompasses your feminine self.

Chapter 8 Questions: God as Mother

1. When in your life have you needed God to be Mother?

2. How does using the pronoun "she" for God make you feel?

3. As we explore the three most common attachment styles (below), I want you to ask yourself how you relate to the mother in God within these categories.

4. How have you attached to your own mother and ultimately how have you attached to God as a parent?

The three main attachment styles are:

- *Secure/Autonomous Attachment*: children have more basic trust; more resiliency, can cope with setbacks and recover more quickly.

- *Avoidant/Dismissive Attachment*: carry anger and anxiety unconsciously; build defenses against perceiving emotional information; displaced aggression and more non-compliance.

- *Ambivalent/Preoccupied Attachment*: no room for having a mind of one's own; have difficulty regulating the expression of negative emotions.

SECTION 3: Dying and Burying

A Menopausal God

I don't like to call them hot flashes, I prefer the term *power surges*.

—MARY CHRISTINE ANTHONY, my mom

Empty Nesting

THE OAK WOOD KITCHEN is quiet. She loads the dishwasher while worship music plays in the background. It had been a beautiful, full weekend with her grown kids all home from college, but they were too soon each headed back in their separate ways, back to their own lives. Her husband had left for work at 8:15 AM, as he had for the past thirty-two years. She exhales. *What will I do with my life now that motherhood is slowed down?* She thinks of her art studio in the backyard. She hasn't been in there to paint for more than a few hours in the past twelve years. Her all-consuming task as mother has shifted, and she is settling into her empty nest. Much of a younger woman's life is determined by how her body is looked at and the level of objectification to her physical beauty. And to the young mother, her every minutes are consumed by the needs of her children. For many women, this season of aging often has been described as the feeling of disappearing and becoming invisible. Because a woman learns to navigate this world in relationship to her body, she must relearn the process of engaging her voice in the final season of her life.

Studies show that the average woman reaches menopause by the age of fifty-two and that lower socioeconomic areas report women reaching menopause as early as age forty-three.[1] Richard Rohr writes about this season of life as "falling upward." He observes that first half of our life is about building a strong "container" made up of rites of passages, marking, gains, and losses. He explains that "the task with the second half of life is to take what we have been given and learn how to deliver it."[2] In other words, the container we built in the beginning of our life holds all that we are to birth in the second half of our life. This is a new season for women, a postpartum one of sorts. Psychological well-being is shown to be high among menopausal women who have marked gains and losses throughout their lives.[3]

Life-Span of the Womb

No matter how gray and rainy the Seattle sky might be, for over five years of Wednesday afternoons, you could find me in a chipper mood crossing the beautiful but soggy campus of Seattle University. As I settle into my dry classroom, I let soft music play as I begin to draw graphs and notes on the dry erase boards around the perimeter of the classroom. On Wednesdays, I teach one of my favorite classes, "Human Growth and Development," otherwise called "Lifespan." There are so many things I enjoy about counseling theories in the lifespan, but my favorite is the lifespan of the female womb and how it illustrates a timeline filled with wonders, anguish, and the mystery of cyclical life and death.

Psychology implores us to observe physiological patterns, such as the fact that when a baby girl is in utero she has about 6 million egg cells in her body, and when she is born she will still have around 2 million egg cells. In the first ten to thirteen years of life, her growing body will absorb almost 1.5 million egg cells, leaving about 400,00 eggs in her ovaries. As a young girl reaches puberty, her body will begin by budding breasts, followed by pubic hair, and finally axillary hair. Once the female body produces axillary hair, within a few months, a girl will begin her menstrual cycle.[4] There are only about 400 eggs that will actually go through the ovulation process. If we continue to follow the woman's body, we see that after ten years of practicing ovulation, she will reach her peak decade for reproduction. Reproduction will span a woman's mid-twenties to mid-thirtiess, encompassing

1. Palacios et al., "Age of menopause."
2. Rohr, *Falling Upward*, 1.
3. Baltes and Baltes, "Psychological perspectives."
4. Broderick and Blewitt, *The Life Span*.

but not limited to: infertility, miscarriage, stillbirth, birth, postpartum, and breastfeeding. During a woman's late thirties to early forties, she moves into a stage called senescing, which means growing down. Female climacteric is the critical and final stage in the uterus's development in a woman's body. The most common example is menopause, which is the natural biological change in a woman's menstrual cycle that signals that the ability to reproduce is ending. Climacteric is specific to the uterus senescing; the womb will gradually lose the ability to reproduce because of a decrease in the circulation of estradiol and estrogen.[5]

The lifespan of this one organ echoes to us that the heart of our Creator longs for humans to create. This cycle of creating something is more complex than we ever imagined; it requires seasons of growth, risk, failure, and success. Creating is an intimate process that requires incredible vulnerability. Our Creator desired for us to co-create with him. God is a God who wants life, and don't limit this idea to physical life alone; it is so much larger than just a human life. God invited all humans to take part in creating, because our God is an ever-bearing God. Our loving God has made every creature ever-bearing with hopes that we will worship by creating life everywhere we are. Whether this is spiritual, emotional, or physical life, there is a cycle we can engage in with God as we co-create. This cycle, which includes everything from hope and celebration to trauma and loss, is studied in the psychological process of gains and losses throughout our lifetime.

Marking: Gains & Losses

Over each of our lifespans, our life cycle will have gains and losses. Our losses increase as we grow older; these losses begin to increase in the later thirties to mid-forties and spike significantly after age seventy until death. How we manage increased losses in our aging life will often mirror how we marked the gains in our adolescent life. Earlier in the chapters on menarche, we talked about rites of passage, which are indicators of how we marked significant moments in our life. Rites of passage are described as marking an important stage in one's life or an event associated with crisis or change of status: especially birth, puberty, or illness. How did we come to celebrate rites of passage such as naming, coming of age, graduations, leaving home, weddings, birthing children, empty nesting? If this is done in an intentional and healthy way, a person can look to their story and see times of marking

5. Boulet et al., "Climacteric and menopause."

or making meaning of both gains and losses in our lives. In many cultures, marking is done through intentional actions that we participate in to make meaning of different events in our lives: a baptism, quincinera, bar mitzvah, wedding, or funeral. Rites of passage, ceremonies, and rituals are all historical ways humans have engaged our bodies as we grow older. Research shows that marking and finding meaning impacts how we cope later in life with the increased losses that we inevitably encounter. [6]

This life cycle of increased gain followed by increased loss is easily seen in parallel to the life cycle of the woman's womb. The womb moves through the stages of ovulation and reproduction, which comprise our season of significant gains, and finally comes to the stage of menopause, to our season of increased loss. [7] In the season of senescing, the womb goes to sleep and at the death of a woman, she is remembered by her legacy. [8] God created the womb to leave an everlasting legacy through the birth of another female who carries a womb. In every female body is a womb that carries eggs and every woman gives a "x" chromosome that creates another female who will continue her legacy with the womb filled with eggs her mother gives her. The life cycle of one's ovaries and uterus were created with the potential to birth a life that would, in most cases, continue to bring forth more life, even after her death. For example, a woman who has a daughter gives life to an ever-bearing life. A womb that creates another female leaves a legacy.

Cyclical Theology and Life Cycles

My sweet boy's hands are shaking with excitement as he shows me the project he has been working on for weeks now at school. I look slowly and deliberately at each page of the book he has compiled and read aloud to him the words he has carved out. The book is on the subject of the life cycle of an apple tree: seeds, tree, bud, flower, and fruit. His pages contain seeds and drawings, which he explains with great detail. His voice holds such wonder at the cycle of life. My forty-year-old body is very aware of the life cycle, as it has spent the last decade navigating pregnancies and births. All life is cyclical. Our produce moves from seed to bud to flower to fruit; our planet spins on its axis each day and rotates around the sun each year; our seasons move through spring, summer, autumn, and winter.

6. Hawkley et al., "Stress, aging, and resilience."
7. Carstensen et al., "The resilience of the aging self."
8. Palacios et al., "Age of menopause."

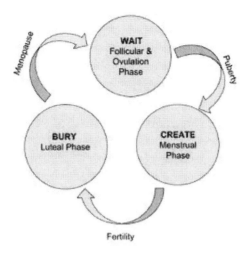

These life cycles are all interconnected, and miraculously so. For humans, the female body bears and illustrates the power of the life cycle. The female body is birthed, grows into puberty, on to fertility and pregnancy, and then menopause. There is a cyclical pattern to the lifespan and, in particular, the lifespan of the uterus or womb. The uterus is an organ held in a woman's body that will naturally cycle through three stages in its lifetime: adolescing, a decade for practicing ovulation; procreation, a decade for peak reproduction; and senescing, a decade of climacteric.[9] In other words, when we observe the lifespan of a uterus in a woman's body, the uterus will grow, menstruate, reproduce, and eventually die. A woman's body bears another cycle every twenty-eight days, and much like the twenty-four hours from sunrise to sunrise tells us a story of creation, the uterus tells a story monthly through the female cycle. If we look to these cycles and study the phases, we see that the Creator was trying to explain to us again and again the process of creation. When God created woman, he tucked in the core of her being an organ that is capable of creating human life. God designed the uterus to convey God's image as Creator. This organ tells us a story in its life, in the cycles it undergoes every month. The female uterus is the part of the body that illustrates the *imago Dei* through the process of creating. We will compare the cycle of the uterus with the cycle of creation; the God as Creator, demonstrated by women as co-creators with God and man to bring human life into this world.

9. Oldenhave et al., "Impact of climacteric."

There are four phases in the monthly cycle of the uterus: menstruation (day one to five), follicular phase (day six to thirteen), ovulation phase (day fourteen) and luteal phase (day fifteen to twenty-eight). Imagine these phases as being parallel to the story God has created on this earth for his people. The sacred text of Genesis 1 illustrates these phases within the creation story: light and darkness, water and land, male and female animals, and finally the human, both body and soul. Science gives a technical breakdown of the hormones and actions in each phase, but in essence, there is a phase in which one must: birth (menstrual), wait (follicular), consummate (ovulation), and bury (luteal).

The circle has long been known as one of the most powerful symbols representing wholeness and cyclical movement. Mercury Trismegistus says, "God is a circle whose center is everywhere and whose circumference is nowhere."[10] We often use the circle as a way of coming together in power, such as a when we gather into a circle to pray. The crown of thorns that Jesus Christ wore on the cross is the most powerful circle to ward against evil; those who work in spiritual warfare use the power of the blood that Christ shed on the cross as their foundation of healing.

These cycles are not only found in the metaphysical life; they also are biblical and correspond to the life of a believer, for example:

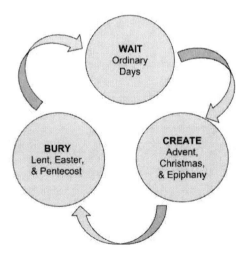

10. Trismegistus, *Miscellaneous Notes*, 3.

When our way of living is examined through a cyclical lens, we find that our bodies and, in particular, a woman's uterus, work in a consistent rotation. With earthly eyes we can easily see the changing of seasons, and with spiritual eyes we can understand the cyclical holy days in the church calendar. Consequently, from a bio-psycho-spiritual understanding, we can see that the female body invites us to uncover a cyclical pattern that can help clarify concepts of spiritual, psychological, and physical interconnectedness.

Chapter 9 Questions: A Menopausal God

1. How do you mark gains and losses in your life?

2. How do you celebrate and how do you grieve?

3. How do you see life cycles in your own story and what themes do they hold for your story?

10

Womb Theology

We cannot taste resurrection until we
have drunk deeply from the cup of suffering.

—Andrew J. Bauman, *Stumbling Toward Wholeness*

The Life, Death, Life Theology of Holy Week

These cycles of life and death are seen both in the natural and spiritual
world. We wait, create, and bury again and again in life. The church, or
bride of Christ, follows this pattern in the ecclesiastical calendar: Ordinary
Time, Advent, Christmas, Epiphany, Lent, Easter, and Pentecost. Even
further, within each holy day or feast, we can distinguish a life/death/life
pattern, such as Christ's Passion and Resurrection through Holy week:
Maundy Thursday, Good Friday, Holy Saturday, and Resurrection Sunday.
Just as we follow these events cycled through these seasons, the womb also
circles through stages: adolescing, reproduction, and senescing. The final
cycle of the womb is called climacteric, the place where the womb falls
asleep or dies. The womb no longer creates physical life but stops bleeding
and ends. We see how a theology erupts from this process; we find that
Christ follows a process to death and we are invited to examine the death of
a woman's womb and the theology integrated within this pattern. The connection of the theology of the womb is played out not only in the manger
scene and the birth of a Savior; it also is represented in the story of the cross,

which we replicate in the sacrament of Communion. Christ demonstrates his greatest teaching ritual still practiced today, Holy Communion, which represents the life/death/life cycle through the act of dying and resurrection. Holy Week is made up of: Maundy Thursday, washing and blessing; Good Friday, crucifixion and death; Holy Saturday, wonder and waiting; and finally, Resurrection Sunday, rebirth and everlasting life. If there ever was a place in the church calendar where the woman's womb cycle is ritualistically acted out, it is here. The womb imitates the cycle of Holy Week: Maundy Thursday (preparation), Good Friday (bleeding), Holy Saturday (waiting), and Resurrection Sunday (life).

Maundy Thursday: Preparation

Raindrops fall lightly on the lower part of my exposed back. I am buckling my daughter into her car seat and my rain jacket has flipped up in the wind. The gray sky is ominous and the chilling air cuts through my layers. As I rush into the driver's seat and shut the door, I see an elderly woman slowly making her way down the sidewalk past my car. I have seen her before: in fact, I probably see her every morning as I drop my son off at school. She has to be in her late eighties if not early nineties. Her wispy gray hair and hunched back are conspicuous as she shuffles her walker down the sidewalk. About eight months ago, the first time I saw her, I offered to help her, but she declined, saying she was walking to the chapel just half a block away. Every time I see her I cringe a bit. I want to tell her to get out of the cold rain, that she might catch pneumonia in this weather and she should really stay inside because she could die out here. Truth is, I don't think she has anything more to live for than her daily walk to the chapel. Her tenacity and faithfulness disturb me in a good way. I want her to be careful and she is obviously not in need of my concern; she wants to be at that prayer service, she wants to be with Jesus. Her bravery to walk two blocks every morning in the cold, gray rain is impressive and stirs an awe in me that I want to have or used to have; either way, I am taken with her commitment. Her spirit has surrendered to live committed to the end, surrendered to the time of waiting that comes during the dying process. I fear my age group has fewer tenacious and warrior-like female role models. If I can be honest, in watching her I am awakened to my own desire to be mentored by a wild and ancient sage. *Sage femme* (or *wise woman*) is a term gifted often to women who work in midwifery, and I long to be parented and impacted by wise women. God often associates as a midwife and I can feel my hunger to understand that idea from an older woman. So, now after I drop my son off at school, I sit with my daughter in the car and we watch this silent saint as she walks to prayer in the blustery weather. We watch her shuffle with her walker in her raincoat as she makes her way to the chapel. I let each laborious step challenge and impact my heart and my spiritual dryness. I want to bear witness to her daily devotion and her arthritic commitment to prayer. I let her teach me. Then as soon as I see the heavy wooden chapel door close, I turn the car on and I go back to my daily schedule.

The process of dying is a courageous act, it is the falling asleep of the body while the mind is still awake. In aging, we can often no longer drive, go to the bathroom on our own, nor do the physical things we once were able to do. As the discipline of waiting for death, aging invites us into the practice of rhythm and faithfulness. Much like my wise mentor who hobbles on winter mornings down the street to the chapel for prayer, this waiting invites us to be relentless in our hope for what is to come.

Maundy Thursday: Theology

Gratitude, blessing, and recognition for those who give of themselves is what Jesus exemplified on Maundy Thursday at the Last Supper. He washed his disciples' feet, broke bread, and drank wine. Maundy Thursday, or Covenant Thursday, means "commandment," illustrating the Last Supper Christ shared with his disciples, and what scholars believe to be the institutionalization of the Eucharist. Christ goes to his beloved disciples, washes their feet, breaks bread, and shares drink with them. I can't help but think he may have hoped they would be loyal and faithful, to walk with him the entire Via Dolorosa, the way of suffering, the way to the cross. Whether or not the disciples will be with Jesus during his darkest hour, and probably even more because he knows they won't be faithful, he washes their feet and offers his gratitude to them for the community they have shared thus far. I have come to know this loneliness, when one is required to teach their friends how to accompany them through grief. Jesus is not bitter as he washes his friends' feet, he isn't angry that, as he needs to be cared for in his final hour, he is caring for them. I believe he genuinely felt gratitude for their friendships, and was truly thankful of their willingness to remain with him. Maundy Thursday invites the follower of Christ to prepare to walk alongside the struggle of the coming death. The events of Holy Week invite women to engage their wombs in the pattern of the Life, Death, and Life cycle that Jesus lives through in Easter season. As women, we can wash ourselves in gratitude as we age, or we can remain silent. The stories of our wombs, the details of how each person spends their lives creating is a beautiful gift to be blessed. Will we bless our bodies for bearing the Life, Death, Life cycle? What does Maundy Thursday look like for your womb? Holy Week on the church calendar is echoed in the cycle of the womb. Christ invites us to walk with him down the Via Dolorosa, the road of suffering, as he makes his way to the cross. Maundy Thursday, Good Friday, Holy Saturday, and Resurrection Sunday play out in the woman's body.

The first day of Holy Week begins with Palm Sunday, yet it is the Maundy Thursday service that invites the church to begin preparation by washing each other's feet and giving thanks for community. Although my home church practices Lent and the stations of the cross, we do not have a Maundy Thursday service. So, annually, our family walks down to the local neighborhood Episcopal Church to participate in communion, washing feet, and receiving blessing. It often holds a few awkward moments, where I vigilantly watch the person in front of me to know what to do; *when do I pour the water, pat dry with a towel my neighbors feet, and do I bless them verbally or say thank you?* These uncomfortable practices invite us into a physical practice, reminding our bodies of the journey Jesus took during this week.

How do we connect this specifically to the womb or the woman's menstrual cycle? I believe the physical act of being given an organ that can create human life is a modern-day miracle. The womb begins at birth producing eggs each month. The cyclical process of menstruation invites every woman to engage her body in an awkward, and many times, undesirable process—just as Jesus' last week before death was marked with suffering. How do we enter into this complexity with curiosity about the Creator of our wombs? Why did God invite all women to co-create with the Creator by giving us a womb? Our uterus is designed to create, and our menstrual cycle is the cyclical reminder of the power our bodies hold. *Women around the world may or may not want to conceive children, but our menstrual cycle reminds us that we have an organ capable of creating life, and the process of creating requires walking through the Via Dolorosa.* The act of shedding blood dates back to the sacrifice required in days of old for a covenant of new life to be enacted.[1] The shedding of blood, which is painful, can be

1. Ramshaw, *The Three-Day Feast.*

an invitation to understand Christ's suffering as God continues to create eternal life in a world of death. Preparation of the sacrifice is part of the ritual process of covenant sacrifice, and Maundy Thursday is the day of preparation and washing for sacrifice. When the lining of the womb is shed, women are invited to be reminded of the sacrifice it takes to create life.

Jesus begins his walk of suffering on Covenant Thursday. This walk is filled with a longing for companionship and a loneliness of shedding blood for a sacrifice. Women are invited in a small way to bear witness to this covenant process, as illustrated in their bodies. Gratitude is a choice, whether blessing our womb for producing a pregnancy or not. While millions are awed by joy when there is no blood, signifying a pregnancy, there are also thousands of women who have been relieved to see blood signifying they are not pregnant.

The womb is one organ that also helps us know the discipline of waiting. Infertility and miscarriage are evil's ugly hand when it comes to establishing the discipline of waiting. Countless women have waited for the first day of their period to pass with no sign of blood; even more have taken a number of pregnancy tests prior to that day, in hopes of not having to wait to know whether or not they are pregnant. All women who have been pregnant and experienced bleeding during their pregnancy have waited on their wombs to find out if more blood would come. To repeat Dr. Dan Allender, "All pregnant women at any time in their pregnancies are at the mercy of being mocked by blood when they go to the bathroom." Death wants to mock us, and evil knows that it can consume our thoughts with fear while waiting. Two verses come to mind: 1 Corinthians 15:55 states "Oh death, where is thy sting?" and Proverbs 13:12 claims that "Hope deferred makes the heart sick." Both of these are concepts of how waiting is a battleground for your hope. No matter the situation, our uterus invites us into a psychological response to bless or curse our body for its complex and awesome power to bring life or death.

Good Friday: Bleeding and Death

I am walking through the concrete, claustrophobic parking garage of the hospital to meet my husband's brother. My sister-in-law, Julie, has reached her final days on this earth due to a battle with cervical cancer. I have flown out to be with her as she prepares for death. The days are spent in awkward pain as fluid fills her body, and I am given one of the greatest honors to sit next to her bed singing over her the songs we once sang together. I know too well the signs of the end. We speak little, but our eyes communicate so much. She is panting for breath, she struggles to ask for things; usually, she wants to hear how her three children are at home. My spirit feels broken, similar to a place I navigated when I buried my son. How can God ask her to leave her children at such a young age? Birthing death is like any other birth, grueling at best. To prepare her body, we spend many hours massaging her swollen legs and pumping them to help her bedridden body push fluids out. When she goes to the bathroom, I brace myself up against her lower back to support her as she contracts through dying organs, much like contractions through a labor. This experience is one I will never forget. My hands supporting her lower back as she writhes in pain, panting for oxygen as water fills her lungs, she says to me through broken heaves of breath, "Finally sister, we are birthing together." I am stunned at the holiness within such a wrong and overwhelmingly broken moment. She has always been able to see with spiritual eyes, and she guides me as we walk through this birthing of death, her death.

As I say goodbye in the early morning to catch a plane home to my children, I know that I won't see her alive again. I kiss her forehead and baptize her with my tears. She squeezes my hand in gratitude, since she can no longer speak. We both know this is goodbye. The walk down the hospital foyer is disoriented with grief and defeat. Once in my car, I weep with deep heaving for a few minutes before I start the car. I don't want to leave, but I know I have to mark this moment for my own body to process my leaving her. I dig in the purse and pull out a package of crackers and a La Croix. I sit in my rental car in the parking lot of that hospital that I will never return to again, and I let the tears fall as I say the words out loud. "I gave it my all, I really gave it my all, Lord, I tried to help her birth this death you are asking from her." That's all the words that come, this simple confession and communion act. With those words, tears stream down my face. Tears of ending, gratitude, and blessing. I bite into the bread, I crack open the La Croix and drink the lukewarm, carbonated water. I let myself and my confession be covered in this communion. This will be the first of my acts of marking Julie's death; to follow will be more traditional acts by which we mark death, such as lighting a candle on the eve of her death, attending her funeral, the burial, and saying goodbye to her time on this earth. When hope gets broken by the betrayal of death, we can either harden ourselves and turn from the pain or break something and ingest it. In that ingestion of communion, we cyclically step into the submission that we live, and choose to continue to live, in a broken world. As an act of communion, I bless Julie's life and preparation for death while breaking bread and taking drink over the act of ending well. In all endings, I often create a marking that mimics a last supper of sorts, so that my own body will recognize and mark this ending well. Blessing Julie, and myself for helping her usher in death, are the first steps of a good ending.

Good Friday: Theology

Good Friday, or God Friday, was named to signify holiness or pious intent.[2] It is a day that takes so much courage to live through, the day of walking toward our earthly death. After being betrayed, Christ was scourged and beaten, then carried his cross to his death on this day. The day signifies an important step in the process: being broken and breaking; flesh or bread. This day is the foundation of our salvation, as Paul observes at 1 Corinthians 15:1–4, our invitation to the cost of eternal love.

There are a few ways we live through Good Friday within our wombs, the events in which we birth death by infertility, miscarriage, stillbirth, and menopause. The concept of living through death is an obvious one when a woman endures infertility, miscarriage, and stillbirths, yet we often overlook the common climacteric response of the body in menopause, which also signifies Good Friday, when sleep finally takes over and this organ is no longer able to create life. The womb offers us many cyclical examples of death: menstrual bleeding, which signifies life has not been conceived, and menopause, which illustrates that the sleeping womb can no longer create life and that death is coming. Death invites us to engage our bodies in letting go; it is an opportunity to say goodbye. Death steals—unless we demand to participate. Often, we are too sad, too surprised, too hurt, too angry, or too scared to demand death let us participate.

In the present day, a typical Good Friday service will end with everything being removed from the altar, the lit candles in the dark auditorium being extinguished, and everyone leaving the church in silence. It is an eerie experience to listen to a deep booming voice sing, "Were you there when they crucified my Lord?" in a pitch-black room, while the lighted candles are being extinguished. A reverent congregation stands there listening in the dark, "Sometimes it causes me to tremble . . . Were you there when they

2. Ramshaw, *The Three-Day Feast.*

crucified my Lord?" And then all goes silent. The silence eerily reminds us that death is real. The crucifixion signifies that our Savior is dead, our redemption is lost, and our belief of good is triumphed over by evil for a day.[3] The shuffling of feet can be heard as people make their way out of the building in hushed tones and faith feels tenuous and possibly lost for a moment. So, we wait, and some of us find hope as we wait.

Holy Saturday: After the Burial

There are four generations of women packed into one car, waiting for her. No one is really talking because we are still in shock that four days ago, my uncle died of a massive heart attack. The days of shock and sorrow were a whirlwind for all of us, and I am not even sure what words I actually said during the funeral service. Even from my cramped backseat spot in the car, I can see my Nanny Janet standing by her husband's fresh grave site. The drizzling rain seems appropriate for my uncle's sudden death, and I realize no one is aware of the cold or wet, as they are mere shadows in comparison to our family's broken hearts. His death caught us all by surprise just as his failing heart caught his long life by surprise, and we were all cut short in our expectations of what should have been. When she finally opens the door and sits in the waiting passenger seat, the car remains silent. We are not a silent type of family—we are constant talkers—so it is eerie as we drive for a while before Nanny breaks the silence. She says quietly, as if only talking to herself, "I know he isn't in his body anymore, but I didn't want to leave him alone in the ground. We have slept in the same bed for so many years now. I just don't want him to be scared out there, alone." Only a widow knows the loneliness death brings to an empty marriage bed. We often witness the immediate days after death, but few are invited into the season that follows the burial of a body. Few people journey well through Holy Saturday, because it is the day of waiting and longing for resurrection to come.

Holy Saturday: Theology

Holy Saturday is the quiet morning our Lord did not arise. It is the quietest day of the year; the silence of Christ's death has settled in through the darkest night of the year and we awake to no promise. As we wait through each

---

3. Pfatteicher and Messerli, eds., *Manual on the Liturgy.*

passing hour for time to alleviate our sorrow, this is the day hope or despair is formed within our theology.[4] Holy Saturday for the womb is similar. It is the act of senescing, slowing down as the womb has fallen asleep. The theology of Holy Saturday is one of hoping and waiting. How do we walk through life after the burial of our beloved? How are we found in our waiting? We wait for what is to be rebirthed. Something was being cultivated in believers' hope as Jesus lay in the tomb. The few beloved remaining followers of Jesus were waiting, watching, and hoping for the promise that death would not reign.

Luke 23:54 names Holy Saturday as a day of waiting, when Jesus' body would have remained in the grave throughout Saturday. The parallel with the womb is that after it births life or death, it must wait, much like soil that needs to replenish before a new seed is sown. It must remain in the grave, for the womb this is either in the season of postpartum or post-menopause. After Christ's most loving act of birthing his death on the cross, the season comes to rest and wait, the day the Spirit prepared Christ's body for resurrection.

Resurrection Sunday: Life and Holiness

The blanket I am wrapped up in on my couch is so cozy that I consider not going at all to the midnight service. The warm, sleeping house is combating my reasoning for saying "yes" to my girlfriend and taking our four-year-old sons to a midnight Easter service. It sounded like a great idea in the park yesterday, waking up our little boys on an adventure that would invite them into the mystery of greeting Resurrection Sunday with great anticipation. I spent many a midnight hour awake waiting for college football game tickets, the first showings of *Star Wars* and *Harry Potter*; why not for Jesus defeating death? It seems that is the greatest event to ever witness. The cold night air wakens me as I carry my sleeping son in his pajamas and put him in the car. We are driving for about fifteen minutes before I hear his voice squeak over the hum of our car engine, "Mom, where are we going?" The excitement and exhaustion can be heard simultaneously in my voice, as I say, "We are going to wait for Jesus to defeat death." When we reach the church, we grab small candles encircled by thin, white paper cones from the table right inside the door. The Greek Orthodox church is packed with people dressed in their Sunday best. I am somewhat embarrassed that my son and

---

4. Brown, *A Crucified Christ in Holy Week.*

I are the only ones in pajamas, but no one seems to notice, and we find our friends who have saved us a seat. The service is completely in Greek and I try to sing along in this foreign tongue, but the smoke of incense catches in my throat. We listen to the songs and chanting for almost an hour before cloth is torn in two, the lights go dim, and the room becomes completely dark. The leaders light a candle and begin walking down the aisles lighting each of our candles. It felt like a reversal of the Good Friday service we usually attend, for with newly lighted candles *light was entering back into the darkness*. Surprisingly, we take our lit candles to the streets and begin a long walk through the neighborhood at one o'clock in the morning. We end the service by sharing a meal. On the way home, I can hear my little boy repeat words he heard at the end of the service, it brings chills to my heart.

"The Lord has risen. He is alive. Death no longer has the final say."

Little did he know those whispered words from my five-year-old boy, would teach his grieving mother. Instead of a church pew, my son ushered me that day through these words to resurrection. Every Easter morning at dawn, for the past six years, since my son Brave died, I find myself at his grave. I struggle going to church on Resurrection Sunday, because my little boy's body is still in the ground. The mother in me feels like a fraud singing songs of resurrection hope; I fear Brave's cold, decaying body will hear them and feel abandoned. This Easter morning feels different, it has only been a few hours since the Orthodox service ended but it is important that I wake again and head to the cemetery. I make my way in the quiet morning fog to Brave's stone marker and kiss it. I look at all the gravestones that cover the grounds, so many bodies waiting for resurrection. The mother in me longs to veer near these waiting bodies, and even more, the mother in me wants to be there in case God picks Resurrection Sunday to come back and raise the dead to life. The passage in John 20 paints a picture of that morning: "Early . . . while it was still dark, Mary Magdalene went to the tomb." There is such love, hope, sorrow and wonder in this verse. Mary Magdalene wanted to be near Christ's body as I want to be near my boy's body. There hasn't been an Easter yet that I have seen the resurrection of all the dead, but I repeat my son's words over his brother's grave: "The Lord has risen. He is alive. Death no longer has the final say." My earthly and heavenly sons are making me a woman of faith.

As believers, death is not our legacy, but rather life.

Resurrection Sunday: Theology

Easter Sunday is the day we celebrate death being defeated and believers receiving eternal life.[5] Such is the story of the womb, for when a woman dies,
if she has birthed at all, the perpetuation of life continues on. In particular
when a womb bears a female womb, it leaves a unique legacy. In the first
months in utero, a female fetus has eggs already tucked inside of her own
reproductive organs. The invitation to co-create life with God is one of the
most intimate experiences I have ever had as a woman: to both create and
birth life. The womb is an exquisite representation of the passageway between the holy and the earthly, the miracle of creation and human life. John
3 speaks of the mystery of being born again, illustrating the new life Jesus
brings by being birthed from the womb. When a woman experiences life
coming out from her own body, she is invited to know God's understanding
of resurrection, new life coming from the earthly tomb.

We hold life and death so closely within the womb. The live kick of
a baby within my belly, the shifting of a shoulder visibly rolling across my
abdomen, is an awe-filling experience. Life waiting to burst out of me, literally, to tear through me and be born. As earlier stated, Old Testament
covenants required blood shed as a necessary part of atonement. We recall
that only a sanctified priest was allowed to enter the veil between the holy
of holies and the outer courts. A bell was tied around the priest's ankle and
a rope dragged behind him in case he was not fit to enter the holiest place,
and thus was struck dead. That heavy-hanging, thickest of cloth veil separated earthly, carnal life, from eternal life and it was ripped down when the
human Savior died and was resurrected. A passageway from death to life.
Matthew 27:51–53 recounts that at Jesus' death the great veil in the temple
was torn by an earthquake. That which separated us from the holy place
was torn in two. There was no longer an eternal separation between life and
death. The female body invites us to understand this concept when a soul
is birthed into this world. God allows women to tell the story through the
theology of their wombs.

5. Ramshaw, *The Three-Day Feast.*

Chapter 10 Questions: Womb Theology

1. How have you come to the places your body is "growing down" or dying?

2. Where do you believe resurrection has shown up in your life after the deaths of your dreams?

3. Do you live in Maundy Thursday (preparation), Good Friday (death), Holy Saturday (waiting), or Easter Sunday (resurrection) the majority of the time?

4. How would Christ find you living here on Earth, between the garden and the grave? What season are you currently in?

11

Climacteric

To continue to live in the hearts of those we leave behind is not to die.

—THOMAS CAMPBELL

A Very Good Day

The small Pensacola airport is quiet on this Wednesday morning. I quickly grab a rental car while explaining to the attendant I am only here for a mere eighteen hours to spend the day on the beach with my grandparents. She stares at me in awe, upgrades my car while she begins to tell a story of her aunt, who she didn't get to say goodbye to before her death. Our culture is hungry to tell of souls who still occupy our hearts but not our world. I am often struck at the longing people have to speak of loved ones who are gone, especially the stories that don't have the end chapters. *Our earthly souls get no greater gift from death than a good goodbye.*

The national park of Navarre Beach is twenty miles of beachside driving with a speed limit of 25 mph to protect nesting shorebirds. I am giddy with excitement to see my grandparents as I drive the peaceful slow-paced road, and the ocean is breathtaking. In a moment of sheer unadulterated whimsy, I pull over and run through the sand until I get to the water. The ocean is clear, blue, and beckoning me to jump in. I take off my red-eye flight-worn dress and tights, and walk deeper into the ocean until I can taste the salty water on my lips, then I submerge. I let the water baptize me in my desired differentiation, as I know I am walking into one of the *last* great moments I will have with my grandparents. Back in the car, I pull onto the slow-paced road and drive until I find the hotel where my family is staying. This day continues to surprise me with goodness as I relish sitting on the shaded porch with my grandparents, and have the honor to help navigate their fragile, aged bodies down to the beach and into the ocean. This day of goodness concludes with a beautiful family dinner and conversation of blessing and love. The night ends with my sister and I cuddling on the couch with both grandparents. As we sit there, we let our heads rest on their chests and listen to their hearts tiredly beating. We all know this is a holy moment, one of the last moments of rest with them, and with brave desperation, our hands all clasped together until exhaustion invites us to sleep. I kissed them all goodnight and promised to see them in four weeks for Father's Day. We always hold our gazes a little longer at each goodbye. We hope for the next visit, but we aren't naive; we know it may never come. My grandmother holds my face and whispers, "I am so glad you came. It was a very good day."

"A very good day," I repeat.

After only a few hours of sleep, I awake before the sun and take in the morning waves before heading back to the airport. The past eighteen hours feel like a dream. I revel in their goodness as I traverse the beautifully scenic beach road. It's time to go home, but how indebted I am to the goodness of yesterday. I will bear the ache of carrying it into a future without them. To mark is to give credence to or to place a symbol for remembrance. Marking something is making meaning in the present moment that will influence the way we remember in the future. Implicit and explicit memory are large indicators in our brain that relay a future pattern of how we adapt. The gift of resilience comes from our ability to adapt to gains and losses in our lives through regulation. I have learned to allow my body to experience the most extravagant memories with those who are birthing life or death, for this act has offered me the kindness I need to regulate and adapt when future loss occurs.

Marking the Last Times

It is four weeks later, and I walk into his familiar living room. He pats his chest with tears in his eyes. "And when I heard you were coming," he pauses to catch his breath and tame his overwhelming emotion, "it made my heart so happy." My grandfather is a man of deep sentiment with a heart of gold. His ninety-four-year-old frame still resembles the strength of his younger years. We are both aware as we talk that we don't have a decade of Father's Days left to share. So, the 3,000 miles we have learned to let live between us is traveled joyfully, because two mornings of waking up to his familiar face are worth it. The smell of the house meets me before I find their faces, their marriage of seventy-seven years is well marked on the path from the garage door, through the dining room, to the living room area. There in their matching light mahogany-pink recliners, you will find them sitting together. My ninety-years-plus pillars of stability, that I find myself leaning on more often than I would like to admit. My grandparents and I will spend these coveted hours looking at pictures of old and telling stories. I ask questions of the future, memorizing their insights and wisdom. Before the day ends, we dream up a project to replicate a photograph that was taken more than thirty years ago. We dig through closets like adventurous excavators for these old clothes we had worn so many years ago. We dress the grandchildren in decade-old clothes and pose them under the orange tree in the backyard. Then we take the film into grandpa's darkroom to develop the pictures, the same darkroom where I spent so much of my adolescent years. I stand in the small room and close my eyes, remembering the smell of stop bath, the ticking of the glowing timerclock, and the timeless framed photograph of my grandmother we developed together years ago. It has all changed over the years. I am watching my grandparents as they accept the inevitable, a submission to death. Preparing for death, accepting an aging body, and stepping into the last stage of life is one of the bravest acts of anyone's life. Senescing is the act of growing downward, where the body begins to shut down and it becomes harder for the dying person to exist with a younger generation that is continuing to grow up. The older soul becomes inner focused as their body slows down and there is little interest in things of life.

Homecare and Senescing

92-year-old, female, Dementia, likes watching Dr. Oz, loves Cheez-its, lives at home with husband (93).

91-year-old, male, Parkinson's, enjoys Big Band music, aspirates on food but loves foot massages, with Hospice Care now.

93-year-old, male, pacemaker and heart at 78% functionality, drives to Walmart once a week, loves cheesecake.

100-year-old, female, healthy and opinionated, lives at home, family checks on her daily, she loves fried chicken.

89-year-old, female, lives in assisted living, no family nearby, used to write scripts for Days of Our Lives, loves rhubarb pie and needs Miralax daily.

These are what my personal notes looked like when I worked for a homecare company for a few years while earning my doctoral degree. I loved my "caseload," these incredible lives that I was paid to care about. It was my favorite thing to remember the little details of each individual so that I could help their last few years of life be comforting and enjoyable. These chicken-scratched notes were so special to me, because they reminded me of the humanity of each of these beloved souls. I spent my days and nights chopping and carrying in firewood, making meals and dispensing medication, bracing frail bodies in the dark on the way to the bathroom, and listening to stories of old. It was an honor to be so close to people during the bravest season of their lives. Aging exposes us, and death is not for the weak of heart. The elderly are my heroes, as I can't imagine all the strength it takes to live through senility. The kindness of these precious people who let me massage their feet, hold their hands during their last breaths, and tend to their bodies at the end and after life; these are my heroes who taught me so much in my own life. It was one of the most rewarding jobs I have ever had before becoming a therapist and mother. My knowledge of death is sadly extensive for someone of my age. My son Brave's death taught me about how to bury and my grandmother, Mema's life taught me about senescing or growing into death.

Growing into Death

The bathroom mirror catches my naked silhouette unflatteringly and I turn quickly to assess. There are four small Band-Aids that starkly remind me of the blood drawn, the glucose test, and the immunizations received on my lunch-break doctor appointment earlier today. I trace the stretch mark lines on my expanded belly while waiting for the bath to fill. Work ended late and Andrew has put the kids down, so I pick up the remaining bath toys as I anticipate the warm water submersion. I will be getting on a four-day train ride first thing in the morning. I push away the thought as I sprinkle Epsom salt in the tub. I don't want to go on this trip. I already have the restriction of not flying during pregnancies after so many miscarriages following altitude changes. The luxury of no kids for this seventy-two-hour train ride is impeded by the reason for this trip. Mema fell yesterday and after multiple staples in her head she lays in ICU fairly unresponsive. In her early nineties, she has earned the right to be unresponsive after such a fall and I have been preparing myself for this moment for the past ten years. Her death will be one of my life's largest blow. She did respond to my name, which is why I will go to her, traveling from Seattle to Louisiana by train to possibly see her one last time.

Almost forty years ago now, if you walked into her yellow flower paper-walled kitchen, you would find me as a young child trying to catch rainbows on her floor. Mema would be standing near the sink window gently moving a small prism back and forth in the sunlight. Those younger years would turn into my sitting on the counter as she cooked, both of us reading through *Jane Eyre* and discussing what it means to learn to love. What follows is an aging woman who would sit for hours in her rocking chair as we had tea, talking about whatever ache was ailing my tender heart. This small window into our relationship will give some insight to why Mema's death will alter me. She has anchored me like no other woman, no other mother, no other grandmother. More than I can express, I want the gift of helping her enter into death. It would be God's greatest kindness to offer me this moment, as Mema has rarely left me alone in my deepest sadness. I would love the opportunity of being with her in her death. It looks like that will probably not be granted to me, yet I board the train in hopes that I can be near her somehow.

In the third trimester of my sixth pregnancy, after she fell, I board the train for four days in hopes I will get there while she is still alive. When I make it to the hospital, a week after her fall, she is sitting up in the chair after an intense fifteen minutes of rehabilitation; she looks like death. She has been staying in a hospital room for over five days now, and I will sleep in the recliner next to her, for the next three nights. In my extremely pregnant condition, there had been little sleep on the train and now I am getting up with her multiple times through the night. We are two hobbling creatures during this season of our lives, my swelling body helping her with IVs, swallowing pills, bathing, and bathroom duties. I dare not say I am exhausted, as she is the one facing this season of death. I know these places of death all too well, and my body just kicks into gear. I have come for this honor, to facilitate helping her body welcome death. It is hard to prepare for death in community, as there are always vulnerable moments of weakness, indecency, and pain.

It takes an awkward bravery to protect the peaceful moments too, like when the spiritual volunteer comes in and offers Mema communion. She is so grateful and all three of us bow our heads and say the Lord's Prayer before she is given the body of Christ. After the volunteer leaves, I scoot closer near her chair and silently pray. She is weeping, and I can't begin to imagine what it is like to receive communion for possibly the last time. After many minutes of silence, a song comes to my heart, and I begin to sing it over her as she weeps. The holiness of that moment outweighs the other harrowing and painful ones. We all deserve to have an advocate in our dying days, one who facilitates and protects the sacred and holy moments along the journey to our last breath. When the song and tears end, we hold each other, and I ask her what it is like to take communion so close to death. We engage in a conversation that will stay with me for the rest of my life.

Birthing Death

The work it takes to die holds many similarities with the work it takes to bring life into this world. Think about the process of birth flipped around for the process of death in an elderly person. With birthing life, the first years of an infant's life are consumed mostly by eating, sleeping, and excreting. A parent is up multiple times in the night feeding, cleaning, rocking, and changing a small baby; aiding her to keep growing. In birthing death, there is a similar pattern to the last years of life for an elderly body coming to death: eating small meals, sleeping often, and the work of excreting. An adult child caring for their dying parent is invited full circle to the sacrifice they once demanded from their parents as an infant: to feed, clean up after, endure sleepless nights, and change diapers. If we follow the process backwards, in the early stages of a newborn, the infant eats very small amounts of milk for the first few days, and the dying body eats little but maybe ice chips in the last few days. Before birth, we are in utero for nine months as the organs form and begin working, adolescing, the body growing up. In the very last stages of death, our bodies shrink, and our organs slow to a stop, senescing or growing down. Anyone who has had to parent a newborn also knows the ways of preparing a body for death. God was intentional to invite loved ones to help care for dying humans, teaching the discipline of growing up into life and growing down into death. I have had to bury more people than I would have liked in my lifetime. I know what it means to pay respects at the wake, to walk up and look at the open casket. Whether closed or open caskets, an urn or memorial, death invites us to birth death and let go. I have attended funerals where fake money is burned, gold coins cover the eyes of the corpse, and gifts are left in the grave for the next life. Most funeral ceremonies have similar procedures: paying respect to the body, the smell of incense waved in a funeral procession, a prayer and eulogy, a processional of headlights to the cemetery, and a burial service. Yet a funeral ceremony is not what I am talking about when I discuss how to facilitate or usher in death. When someone is comfortable with death, they are aware of the intention that happens when death comes to take a life. Death is the absence of someone's earthly existence, the absence of a soul's presence. How have you come to facilitate birthing death?

Initially when one is given the honor to help facilitate death, one must first engage and prepare the body. Homecare and hospice are the two Western organizations most commonly enlisted in the business of preparing individuals and their families for death. When we engage the process, we are invited as individuals to partake in these acts: touching, washing, grooming, speaking, or singing. We begin with touching; we can hold someone's hand, embrace them, lay next to them in a hospital bed, massage their hands or feet, or stand next to them. Washing or grooming can be a more intimate experience, where one washes the dying person's face, hands, or feet to prepare the body for death, as death is not an easy smell to endure. Grooming might include helping them complete bodily functions as their body fails and it becomes harder to do on their own. Speaking over and singing over may consist of any words, prayers, or songs that you might offer the soul before it leaves the body. Everyone can do this differently and there is no script, it is just an invitation to decide how we want to engage the one who is saying goodbye, and to what extent we want to be a part of that process. Ushering in death is not only about advocating for a sacred moment and preparing the body to expire, it is also about saying goodbye well.

Saying Goodbye Well

The house is quiet as I unlock the front door. It is close to midnight, and my grandpa is sleeping over at the hospital with my grandma to give me a break from night duty. The familiar smell of their goodness meets me at the laundry room door as I quickly throw a load of clothes in the wash. As exhausted as I am, I know this is a holy invitation. This is probably the last time I will set foot in their home while they both live in it. The gravity of the moment overwhelms me, and I don't want to move, because if I do, I know it will have to end. As I turn on the light in the darkroom and look at all the pictures of my grandparents through the years, the tears start falling. I let them come freely. My fingers run across the timeless wallpaper as I carry myself through the house and to the kitchen. I am desperate to capture it all, to bottle up inside of me so I don't lose it. As I take silent videos with my phone, I feel the insatiable hunger to tighten my grip and panic. *It is hard to let go of deep goodness. It is difficult to birth death well.* I turn my phone off, sit down in the middle of the floor, and begin to thank the house for the generosity and safety it has brought me through the last forty years. I breathe deeply and tell my body it is time to give thanks and let go. When I feel peace linger long enough, I rock my pregnant body up off the floor and get ready for bed. I go to Mema's room—she had told me to sleep in her bed. The familiar lilac-painted walls, white lace curtains, and crowded dressers welcome me. She hasn't been home since she fell, and I am immediately aware of the blood stains on the carpet and on her shoes near the jewelry box where she fell. I feel afraid to look at them; her life force, her precious blood stained on the ground, but I make myself look. "*I am so sorry, Mema.*" I whisper the words at a barely audible level. I climb into her bed—I will wait until the morning to clean the blood. I remember the tears that came the last time I slept in this bed, but that time she was there with me. I feel gratitude recalling that she sang to me until I fell asleep. This time I repeat the same song she sang over me years ago, and I sing until slumber finds me.

Such is the womb falling asleep to the song of its Mother. Because a woman is made mother by her womb, I beckon us to each learn the song of our womb. This song will teach us the sound to sing when we need to calm, comfort, and aid one through death and birth. I know the song I sang over my children to cover their fretting hearts before sleep; it is the same song I sing over myself when I am in need. The song of a mother is what regulates us, grounds us. Mary, the Mother of God, has come to my mind so often after burying and birthing. I picture her standing near the cross, watching her son dying, every breath getting shallower than the one before. I can imagine the agony she felt watching him die. I can imagine the hopelessness that she that afternoon when the sky went dark and she held his broken and lifeless body in her arms. She had to have had a flashback to the manger when Jesus was born, and he was placed in her arms and put to her breast. The relief and joy of delivering a healthy son in a barn juxtaposes with holding his equally bloody dead body in her arms at the foot of the cross. I often wonder what sound Mary hummed as she held Jesus when he was a newborn, and I wonder if she hummed that same song over him as she held his lifeless body after he was taken off the cross. I imagine her song to be something like this,

Rest my love, my precious one, you are safe now,
you are in your Mother's arms, you are in your Father's arms,
blood and water brought you to me,
blood and water took you from me.
Death is no longer any human's fear, for you have saved us all,
and you already live again.

The theology of the womb is inside each of us. Now you have heard mine, and if you're quiet for but a moment, you will hear your own; for she is humming inside of you.

EPILOGUE

Gracious reader, I am indebted to your bravery to journey through this book. For within your courage to walk through this text with me, I have also come to know God as Mother and God as Sister. I am ever grateful for your sacrifice to create life in this dying world. Thank you for your strength, and may you place your hand on your womb and offer it your gratitude, for our mighty God has invited you to know her in this holy place, your body, your womb. May you realize that the theology of the womb is not confined to the words in this book alone, but each woman, as different and unique as the sunrise and sunset each day, is what makes up the theology of the womb. I beckon you to explore the story of your womb specifically because it holds a theology of God that the world is desperate to know in order to continue to create more life. I am waiting for the uniqueness of your womb's story, my daughter and granddaughters are waiting to hear and read about it as you live your life theology aloud. We are in need of this sisterhood, so that we can know God's likeness as a woman.

I am woman, *imago Dei*, an image bearer of God, chosen to carry a message of creation, death, and ultimately everbearing life.

Bibliography

Section 1

Brown, Brené. *The Gifts of Imperfection: Let Go of Who You Think You're Supposed to Be and Embrace Who You Are.* Center City, MN: Hazelden, 2010.

———. "Shame Resilience Theory: A Grounded Theory Study on Women and Shame." *Families in Society* 87.1 (2006) 43–52.

Buckley, Thomas, and Alma Gottlieb, eds. *Blood Magic: The Anthropology of Menstruation.* Berkeley, CA: University of California Press, 1988.

Choplin, Leslie, and Jenny Beaumont. *These Are Our Bodies: Talking Faith and Sexuality at Church & Home-Foundation Book.* New York: Church Publishing, 2016.

Davies, Claire C., Dorothy Brockopp, Krista Moe, Peggy Wheeler, Jean Abner, and Alexander Lengerich. "Exploring the Lived Experience of Women Immediately Following Mastectomy." *Cancer Nursing* 40.5 (2017) 361–68.

Dearing, Ronda L., and June Price Tangney. *Shame in the Therapy Hour.* 1st ed. Washington, DC: American Psychological Association, 2011.

Eicher, Joanne B., and Lisa Ling. *Mother, Daughter, Sister, Bride: Rituals of Womanhood.* Washington, DC: National Geographic, 2006.

Ezeh, P-J. "Sex, custom and population: A Nigerian Example." *International Journal of Sociology and Anthropology* 6.3 (2014) 105–9.

Farrell, Heather. *Walking with the Women of the Old Testament.* Springville, UT: CFI, 2014.

———. "What Does It Mean for a Woman to be 'Unclean' in the Bible?" Women in the Scriptures, 2016. http://www.womeninthescriptures.com/2016/02/what-does-it-mean-for-woman-to-be.html.

Farson, Richard. *Birthrights.* New York: Macmillan, 1974.

Gottlieb, Alma. "Sex, Fertility and Menstruation among the Beng of the Ivory Coast: A Symbolic Analysis." *Africa* 52.4 (1982) 34–47.

Gottlieb, Erika. *Becoming My Mother's Daughter: A Story of Survival and Renewal.* Life Writing Series. Waterloo, ON: Wilfrid Laurier University Press, 2008.

Gumming, David C., Ceinwen E. Gumming, and Dianne K. Kieren. "Menstrual mythology and sources of information about menstruation." *American Journal of Obstetrics and Gynecology* 164.2 (1991) 472–76.

Harrison-Hohner, J. "Do Women's Cycles Sync Up?" Women's Health, 2010. https://blogs.webmd.com/womens-health/2010/10/do-womens-cycles-sync-up.html.

Huffington Post. "Religion: What is a Mikvah and what does it have to do with Sex?" 2014. https://www.huffingtonpost.com/2014/11/01/what-is-a-mikvah_n_6069556.html.

Janus, Adrienne. "Laughter and the Limits of Identity: Joyce, Beckett and the Philosophical Anthropology of Laughter." *Études irlandaises* 38.1 (2013).

Lane, Belden C. "Mother Earth as Metaphor: A Healing Pattern of Grieving and Giving Birth." *Horizons* 21.1 (1994) 7–21.

Lee, Janet, and Jennifer Sasser-Coen. "Memories of menarche: Older women remember their first period." *Journal of Aging Studies* 10.2 (1996) 83–101.

Lockshin, Shoshana. *Measure of Women's Health*. American Health Rankings, 2016. https://www.americashealthrankings.org/learn/reports/2016-health-of-women-and-children-report/measures-of-womens-health-behaviors.

———. "Mikveh." My Jewish Learning, 2019. https://www.myjewishlearning.com/article/the-mikveh/.

Mölsä, Melissa, et al. "Functional role of P-glycoprotein in the human blood-placental barrier." *Clinical Pharmacology & Therapeutics* 78.2 (2005) 123–31.

Paulsell, Stephanie. *Honoring the Body: Meditations on a Christian Practice*. Practices of Faith. San Francisco: Jossey-Bass, 2002.

Pierce, Yolanda. "Why God Is a 'Mother,' Too." *Time,* November 15, 2013. http://ideas//time.com/2013/05/11/why-god-is-a-mother-too/.

Pretchel, M. *The Smell of Rain on Dust*. Berkeley, CA: North Atlantic, 2015.

Provençal, Nadine, and Elisabeth B. Binder. "The effects of early life stress on the epigenome: from the womb to adulthood and even before." *Experimental Neurology* 268 (2015) 10–20.

Shuler, Brandon D., Johnson, Rob, and Garza-Johnson, Erika. *New Border Voices : An Anthology*. 1st ed. College Station, TX: Texas A & M University Press, 2014.

Simango, Daniel. "The meaning of the imago Dei (Gen 1:26–27) in Genesis 1–11." *Old Testament Essays* 25.3 (2012) 638–56.

Siegel, Daniel J. "Toward an interpersonal neurobiology of the developing mind: Attachment relationships, 'mindsight,' and neural integration." *Infant Mental Health Journal: Official Publication of The World Association for Infant Mental Health* 22.1–2 (2001) 67–94.

Siegel, Daniel J., and Marion Solomon, eds. *Healing Trauma: Attachment, Mind, Body and Brain*. Norton Series on Interpersonal Neurobiology. New York: W. W. Norton, 2003.

Tan, Delfin A., Rohana Haththotuwa, and Ian S. Fraser. "Cultural aspects and mythologies surrounding menstruation and abnormal uterine bleeding." *Best Practice & Research Clinical Obstetrics & Gynaecology* 40 (2017) 121–33.

Van der Kolk, Bessel. *The Body Keeps the Score*. New York: Viking, 2014.

Wenham, G. J. *The International Commentary on the Old Testament*. Grand Rapids: Eerdmans, 1979.

Whitekettle, Richard. "Levitical thought and the female reproductive cycle: Wombs, wellsprings, and the primeval world." *Vetus Testamentum* 46 (1996) 376–91.

Wurn, Belinda, and Larry Wurn, with Richard King. *Overcoming Our Infertility and Pain, Naturally*. Gainesville, FL: Med-Art, 2011. http://www.clearpassage.com/resources/educational-ebooks/.

Sections 2 and 3

Abber, Caitlin, and Nicole Abi-Najeme. "Around the World in 28 Periods." Women's Health, 2015. https://www.womenshealthmag.com/life/periods-around-the-world.

Al-Ghazal, S. K., L. Fallowfield, and R. W. Blamey. "Comparison of psychological aspects and patient satisfaction following breast conserving surgery, simple mastectomy and breast reconstruction." *European Journal of Cancer* 36.15 (2000) 1938–43.

Baltes, Paul B., and Margret M. Baltes. "Psychological perspectives on successful aging: The model of selective optimization with compensation." *Successful Aging: Perspectives from the Behavioral Sciences* 1.1 (1990) 1–34.

Barker, Kenneth L., John H. Stek, and Ronald F. Youngblood, eds. *Zondervan TNIV Study Bible: Today's New International Version.* Grand Rapids: Zondervan, 2006.

Bell, Rob. *Sex God: Exploring the Endless Connections between Sexuality and Spirituality.* Grand Rapids: Zondervan, 2007.

Bercovitch, Sacvan. "Endicott's Breastplate: Symbolism and Typology in 'Endicott and the Red Cross.'" *Studies in Short Fiction* 4.4 (1967) 289–91.

Biale, David. "The god with breasts: El Shaddai in the Bible." *History of Religions* 21.3 (1982) 240–56.

Boulet, Monique J., et al. "Climacteric and menopause in seven South-east Asian countries." *Maturitas* 19.3 (1994) 157–76.

Bowlby, John. *Attachment.* New York: Basic, 2008.

Brady, Laura. "La Huesera: Articulating the Skeletons of Stories and Essays." In *Questioning Authority: Stories Told in School,* edited by Linda Adler-Kassner and Susanmarie Harrington, 97–101. Ann Arbor, MI: University of Michigan Press, 2001.

Brink, Susan. "Some Cultures Treat Menstruation With Respect." NPR.Org, August 11, 2015. https://www.npr.org/sections/goatsandsoda/2015/08/11/431605131/attention-trump-some-cultures-treat-menstruation-with-respect.

Bretherton, Inge. "The origins of attachment theory: John Bowlby and Mary Ainsworth." *Developmental psychology* 28.5 (1992) 759–75.

Broderick, P., and Pamela Blewitt. *The Life Span: Human Development for Helping Professionals.* Upper Saddle River, NJ: Merrill/Prentice Hall, 2003.

Brown, Raymond Edward. *A Crucified Christ in Holy Week: Essays on the Four Gospel Passion Narratives.* Collegeville, MN: Liturgical, 1986.

Buckley, Thomas, and Alma Gottlieb, eds. *Blood Magic: The Anthropology of Menstruation.* Berkeley, CA: University of California Press, 1988.

Carstensen, Laura, Alexandra Freund, J. Brandtstädter, and W. Greve. "The resilience of the aging self." *Development Review* 14.1 (1994) 81–92.

Carus, Paul. "The Oracle of Yahveh: The Urim and Thummim, the Ephod, and the Breastplate of Judgment." *The Monist* 17.3 (1907) 365–88.

Cozolino, Louis. *The Neuroscience of Human Relationships: Attachment and the Developing Social Brain.* New York: W. W. Norton, 2014.

Desborough, J. P. "The stress response to trauma and surgery." *British Journal of Anesthesia* 85.1 (July 1, 2000) 109–17. https://doi.org/10.1093/bja/85.1.109.

Diamant, Anita. *The Red Tent.* New York: Picador USA, 1997.

Estés, Clarissa Pinkola. *Women Who Run with the Wolves : Myths and Stories of the Wild Woman Archetype.* New York : Ballantine, 1992.

Farley, Margaret. *Just Love: A Framework for Christian Sexual Ethics.* New York: Continuum, 2008.

Flood, M. "The harms of pornography exposure among children and young people." *Child Abuse Review: Journal of the British Association for the Study and Prevention of Child Abuse and Neglect* 18.6 (2009) 384–400.

Fosha, Diana, Daniel J. Siegel, and Marion Solomon, eds. *The Healing Power of Emotion: Affective Neuroscience, Development & Clinical Practice.* New York: W. W. Norton, 2009.

Freedman, Mervin B., et al. "The Interpersonal Dimension of Personality 1." *Journal of Personality* 20.2 (1951) 143–61.

Gendler, A. "Why Do We Cry?: Three Different Types of Tears and Their Physiology." www.Medical.Daily, 2015. http://www.medicaldaily.com/pulse/why-do-we-cry-three-different-types-tears-and-their-physiology-331708.

Greene, John Gerald. "Constructing a standard climacteric scale." *Maturitas* 61.1–2 (2008) 78–84.

Harrison-Hohner, J. "Do Women's Cycles Sync Up?" Women's Health, 2010. https://blogs.webmd.com/womens-health/2010/10/do-womens-cycles-sync-up.html.

Hawkley, Louise C., et al. "Stress, aging, and resilience: Can accrued wear and tear be slowed?" *Canadian Psychology/Psychologie Canadienne* 46.3 (2005) 115–25.

Jacobs, Jennifer E. "Ululation in Levantine Society: The Cultural Reproduction of an Affective Vocalization." PhD diss., available from ProQuest, 2008.

Kuryluk, Ewa. *Veronica and Her Cloth: History, Symbolism, and Structure of a "True" Image.* Oxford: Blackwell, 1991.

Lewis, T. "Breastplate of the High Priest." In *International Standard Bible Encyclopedia*, edited by James Orr, 1–5. Chicago: Howard-Severance, 1915.

Lucas, Alan, et al. "Breast milk and subsequent intelligence quotient in children born preterm." *The Lancet* 339.8788 (1992) 261–64.

MacClancy, Jeremy. "The milk tie." In *Anthropology of Food, Vol. 2: Essays in Honor of Helen Macbeth*, edited by Jeremy MacClancy et al., 163–82. Guadalajara: Universidad de Guadalajara, 2003.

Maclaren, Alexander. *Rev. Dr. Alexander Maclaren's Bible Class Expositions.* Vol. 17. New York: AC Armstrong & Son, 1894.

Madsen, Pamela. "12 Crazy Amazing Facts about the Clitoris." *Huffington Post*, June 27, 2015. https://www.huffingtonpost.com/pamela-madsen/12-crazy-amazing-facts-about-the-clitoris_b_7501188.html.

Mamre, Mechon. "Torah 101: Kosher Sex." https://www.mechon-mamre.org/jewfaq/torah.htm.

The Mayo Clinic. "Miscarriage." https://www.mayoclinic.org/diseases-conditions/pregnancy-loss-miscarriage/symptoms-causes/syc-20354298.

Mennicke, A., D. Anderson, K. Oehme, and S. Kennedy. "Law enforcement officers' perception of rape and rape victims: A multimethod study." *Violence and Victims* 29.5 (2014) 814–27.

The Merriam-Webster Dictionary. Springfield, MA: Merriam-Webster, Incorporated, 2006.

Nelson, Gertrud Mueller. *Here All Dwell Free: Stories to Heal the Wounded Feminine.* Eugene, OR: Wipf and Stock, 1999.

Nelson, Wendy. "Sexuality in Judaism." http://www.mesacc.edu/~thoqh49081/StudentPapers/JewishSexuality.html.

Neumann, I., J. A. Russell, and R. Landgraf. "Oxytocin and vasopressin release within the supraoptic and paraventricular nuclei of pregnant, parturient and lactating rats: a microdialysis study." *Neuroscience* 53.1 (1993) 65–75.

Newsom, Carol Ann, and Sharon H. Ringe, eds. *Women's Bible Commentary.* Louisville: Westminster John Knox, 1998.

Northrup, Christiane. "Women's Wisdom, Women's Bodies." *Your Work is a Godsend.* http://www.clearpassage.com/site-resources/guide-to-services-womens-health.pdf.

O'Donohue, John. *Anam Ćara: A Book of Celtic Wisdom.* 1st paperback ed. New York: Cliff Street, 1998.

Oldenhave, Anna, et al. "Impact of climacteric on well-being: a survey based on 5213 women 39 to 60 years old." *American Journal of Obstetrics and Gynecology* 168.3 (1993) 772–80.

Ozkan, Hasan, et al. "Milk kinship hypothesis in light of epigenetic knowledge." *Clinical Epigenetics* 4.1 (2012) 4–14.

Palacios, S., et al. "Age of menopause and impact of climacteric symptoms by geographical region." *Climacteric* 13.5 (2010) 419–28.

Paulsell, Stephanie. *Honoring the Body: Meditations on a Christian Practice.* Practices of Faith. San Francisco: Jossey-Bass, 2002.

Pfatteicher, Philip H., and Carlos R. Messerli, eds. *Manual on the Liturgy: Lutheran Book of Worship.* Minneapolis: Augsburg Fortress, 1979.

Pierce, Yolanda. "Why God Is a 'Mother,' Too." *Time*, November 15, 2013. http://ideas//time.com/2013/05/11/why-god-is-a-mother-too/.

Pope John Paul II. *Man and Woman He Created Them: A Theology of the Body.* Chicago: Pauline, 2006.

———. *The Theology of the Body: Human Love in the Divine Plan.* Chicago: Pauline, 1997.

Poythress, Vern S., and Wayne A. Grudem. *The Gender-Neutral Bible Controversy : Muting the Masculinity of God's Words.* Nashville: Broadman and Holman, 2000.

Prechtel, Martin. *The Smell of Rain on Dust: Grief and Praise.* Berkeley, CA: North Atlantic, 2015.

Ramshaw, Gail. *The Three-Day Feast: Maundy Thursday, Good Friday, and Easter.* Minneapolis: Augsburg, 2004.

Resnick, Barbara, L. Gwyther, and Karen A. Roberto. *Resilience in Aging.* New York: Springer, 2011.

Rohr, Richard. *Falling Upward: A Spirituality for the Two Halves of Life.* San Francisco: Jossey-Bass, 2011.

Sellers, Tina Schermer. *Sex, God, and the Conservative Church: Erasing Shame from Sexual Intimacy.* New York: Routledge, 2017.

———. "The Vow of Onah and Other Jewish Attitudes about Sex." tinaschermersellers.com, February 2, 2011. http://tinaschermersellers.com/2011/02/12/the-vow-of-onah-and-other-jewish-attitudes-about-sex/.

Shemaryahu, Talmon. "The Desert Motif in the Bible and in Qumran Literature." In *Biblical Motifs: Origins and Transformations*, edited by Alexander Altmann, 37–44. Cambridge, MA: Harvard University Press, 1966.

Siegel, Daniel J., and Marion Solomon, eds. *Healing Trauma: Attachment, Mind, Body and Brain.* Norton Series on Interpersonal Neurobiology. New York: W. W. Norton, 2003.

Siegel, Daniel J. *The Developing Mind.* 1st ed. New York: Guilford, 1999.

Smith-Kirwin, Susan M., et al. "Leptin expression in human mammary epithelial cells and breast milk." *The Journal of Clinical Endocrinology & Metabolism* 83.5 (1998) 1810–1813.

Spurgeon, C. H. *The Treasury of David*. Toronto: Funk and Wagnalls, 1892.

Stevens, Laurie A., et al. "The psychological impact of immediate breast reconstruction for women with early breast cancer." *Plastic Reconstructive Surgery* 73.4 (1984) 619–28.

Strong, James. *The New Strong's Exhaustive Concordance of the Bible: With Main Concordance, Appendix to the main concordance, Hebrew and Aramaic Dictionary of the Old Testament, Greek Dictionary of the New Testament*. Nashville: Thomas Nelson, 1995.

Tippett, Krista, host. "Soul, Food, Sex and Space." *On Being*, March 17, 2016. https://onbeing.org/programs/nikki-giovanni-soul-food-sex-and-space-aug2017/.

Towns, Elmer L. *My Father's Names: The Old Testament Names for God and How They Can Help You Know Him More Intimately*. Ventura, CA: Regal, 1991.

Trismegistus, Mercury. *Miscellaneous Notes and Queries: History, Folklore, Mathematics, Mystics, Arts, Science, Etc*. Vol. XIV. Manchester, NH: Gould, 1896.

Van Der Kolk, Bessel A. *The Body Keeps the Score: Brain, Mind, and Body in the Healing of Trauma*. New York: Viking, 2014.

Victora, Cesar G., et al. "Breastfeeding in the 21st century: epidemiology, mechanisms, and lifelong effect." *The Lancet* 387.10017 (2016) 475–90.

Welsh, J. K., and J. T. May. "Anti-infective properties of breast milk." *The Journal of Pediatrics* 94.1 (1979) 1–9.

Wenham, G. J. *The International Commentary on the Old Testament*. Grand Rapids: Eerdmans, 1979.

Appendix A

Genesis 1 King James Version (KJV)

1 In the beginning God created the heaven and the earth.

2 And the earth was without form, and void; and darkness was upon the face of the deep. And the Spirit of God moved upon the face of the waters.

3 And God said, Let there be light: and there was light.

4 And God saw the light, that it was good: and God divided the light from the darkness.

5 And God called the light Day, and the darkness he called Night. And the evening and the morning were the first day.

6 And God said, Let there be a firmament in the midst of the waters, and let it divide the waters from the waters.

7 And God made the firmament and divided the waters which were under the firmament from the waters which were above the firmament: and it was so.

8 And God called the firmament Heaven. And the evening and the morning were the second day.

9 And God said, Let the waters under the heaven be gathered together unto one place, and let the dry land appear: and it was so.

10 And God called the dry land Earth; and the gathering together of the waters called he Seas: and God saw that it was good.

11 And God said, Let the earth bring forth grass, the herb yielding seed, and the fruit tree yielding fruit after his kind, whose seed is in itself, upon the earth: and it was so.

12 And the earth brought forth grass, and herb yielding seed after his kind, and the tree yielding fruit, whose seed was in itself, after his kind: and God saw that it was good.

13 And the evening and the morning were the third day.

14 And God said, Let there be lights in the firmament of the heaven to divide the day from the night; and let them be for signs, and for seasons, and for days, and years:

15 And let them be for lights in the firmament of the heaven to give light upon the earth: and it was so.

16 And God made two great lights; the greater light to rule the day, and the lesser light to rule the night: he made the stars also.

17 And God set them in the firmament of the heaven to give light upon the earth,

18 And to rule over the day and over the night, and to divide the light from the darkness: and God saw that it was good.

19 And the evening and the morning were the fourth day.

20 And God said, Let the waters bring forth abundantly the moving creature that hath life, and fowl that may fly above the earth in the open firmament of heaven.

21 And God created great whales, and every living creature that moveth, which the waters brought forth abundantly, after their kind, and every winged fowl after his kind: and God saw that it was good.

22 And God blessed them, saying, Be fruitful, and multiply, and fill the waters in the seas, and let fowl multiply in the earth.

23 And the evening and the morning were the fifth day.

24 And God said, Let the earth bring forth the living creature after his kind, cattle, and creeping thing, and beast of the earth after his kind: and it was so.

25 And God made the beast of the earth after his kind, and cattle after their kind, and every thing that creepeth upon the earth after his kind: and God saw that it was good.

26 And God said, Let us make man in our image, after our likeness: and let them have dominion over the fish of the sea, and over the fowl of the air, and over the cattle, and over all the earth, and over every creeping thing that creepeth upon the earth.

27 So God created man in his own image, in the image of God created he him; male and female created he them.

28 And God blessed them, and God said unto them, Be fruitful, and multiply, and replenish the earth, and subdue it: and have dominion over the fish of the sea, and over the fowl of the air, and over every living thing that moveth upon the earth.

29 And God said, Behold, I have given you every herb bearing seed, which is upon the face of all the earth, and every tree, which is the fruit of a tree yielding seed; to you it shall be for meat.

30 And to every beast of the earth, and to every fowl of the air, and to every thing that creepeth upon the earth, wherein there is life, I have given every green herb for meat: and it was so.

31 And God saw every thing that he had made, and, behold, it was very good. And the evening and the morning were the sixth day.

Appendix B

<u>Genesis 1:26-27: Hebrew and Latin</u>

"Then God said, 'Let us make human beings in *our* image, in *our* likeness, so that they may rule over the fish in the sea and the birds in the sky, over the livestock and all the wild animals, and over all the creatures that move along the ground.' So God created human beings in his own image, *in the image of God he created them*; male and *female* he created them."

The Hebrew word for "image" is *tselem* (צֶלֶם), which means "photograph," "resemblance," "figure," or "shadow." The Latin translation is *imago dei*, the "image of God," which I often refer to throughout this book.

Appendix C

Encampment of Tribes of Israel

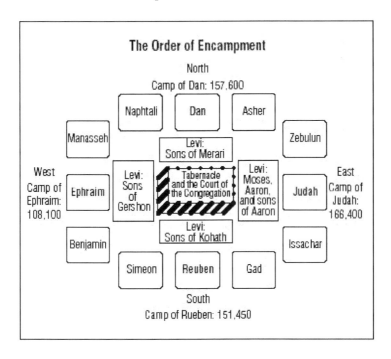

The Order of Encampment

North
Camp of Dan: 157,600

Naphtali | Dan | Asher

Manasseh

Levi:
Sons of Merari

Zebulun

West
Camp of
Ephraim:
108,100

Levi:
Sons
of
Gershon

Tabernacle
and the Court of
the Congregation

Levi:
Moses,
Aaron,
and sons
of Aaron

Ephraim

Judah

East
Camp of
Judah:
166,400

Levi:
Sons of Kohath

Benjamin

Issachar

Simeon | Reuben | Gad

South
Camp of Rueben: 151,450

Appendix D

Cultures which include Singing to Bones.
1. The Singing Bone (Jacob and Wilhelm Grimm).
2. The Singing Bones (French Louisiana).
3. Under the Green Old Oak-Tree (Antigua).
4. The Griffin (Italy).
5. The Dead Girl's Bone (Switzerland).
6. The Little Bone (Switzerland).
7. Binnorie (England).
8. Murder Will Out (Iceland).
9. The Silver Plate and the Transparent Apple (Russia).
10. Little Anklebone (Pakistan).

Made in the USA
Columbia, SC
25 May 2022